Poetry and Consciousness

POETS ON POETRY

David Lehman, General Editor
Donald Hall, Founding Editor

New titles

Recently published

Also available are collections by

A. R. Ammons, Robert Bly, Philip Booth, Marianne Boruch,
Hayden Carruth, Fred Chappell, Amy Clampitt, Tom Clark,
Douglas Crase, Robert Creeley, Donald Davie, Peter Davison,
Tess Gallagher, Suzanne Gardinier, Thom Gunn, John Haines,
Donald Hall, Joy Harjo, Robert Hayden, Daniel Hoffman,
Weldon Kees, Galway Kinnell, Mary Kinzie, Kenneth Koch,
Richard Kostelanetz, Maxine Kumin, Martin Lammon (editor),
David Lehman, Philip Levine, John Logan, William Matthews,
William Meredith, Jane Miller, John Frederick Nims, Gregory Orr,
Alicia Ostriker, Marge Piercy, Anne Sexton, Charles Simic,
Louis Simpson, William Stafford, Richard Tillinghast,
Diane Wakoski, Alan Williamson, Charles Wright, and
James Wright

C. K. Williams

Poetry and Consciousness

Ann Arbor

THE UNIVERSITY OF MICHIGAN PRESS

2001   2000   1999   1998   4   3   2   1

A CIP catalog record for this book is available from the British Library.

Library of Congress Cataloging-in-Publication Data

Williams, C. K. (Charles Kenneth), 1936–
    Poetry and consciousness / C.K. Williams.
       p.   cm.
    ISBN 0-472-09672-9 (acid-free paper). — ISBN 0-472-06672-2 (pbk.
: acid-free paper)
    1. Poetry—History and criticism.   I. Title.
PN1042.W513   1998
809.1—dc21   98-5418
                                                          CIP

Contents

Poetry and Consciousness

Recently I've come to realize that the way I've been taught to describe consciousness to myself doesn't really have much to do with the consciousness with which I experience poetry, either in reading it or trying to write it. Especially in regard to the particular manifestation of consciousness that we call emotion, and that determines, after all, our ultimate judgment of any experience, poetry certainly included, I feel a great deal of conceptual uncertainty. The most abstract idea and the most philosophically sophisticated poem have feelings attached to them; without feeling, there is no resonance, nothing of what we call real meaning, but regarded from the point of view of poetry and mind, the way our culture defines emotion can be uncertain and troubling. Certainly our philosophical and psychological heritage contains a vast enough debate on the mind, but when I actually consider my own mind, particularly the way I experience mind in relation to emotion, I find that although I have learned a great deal from Freud, from James, from Ryle and Wittgenstein, somehow the consciousness and emotional mechanisms with which I live haven't quite been accounted for in any of the systems with which I'm familiar.

To begin with, I've been puzzled for a long time by what exactly an emotion is. I know the *words* for emotions: *love, hate, anger, dread,* and so on, but considering the central position emotions play in our lives, we have a surprisingly small number of terms to describe or embody them, and often we find ourselves

© C. K. Williams. First delivered as a talk to the annual conference of the American Psychiatric Association, 1986; first published in *The American Poetry Review,* 1987.

groping for modifying systems that become overcomplicated and confusing.

Next, even with the terms we do have, we seem to be terribly vague and general in our dealings with emotions. If I say to you, "I am depressed," you will have, we'll both think, a pretty good idea of what I'm feeling. If, on the other hand, either of us wishes to be more specific, if I want to tell you more or if you want to ask more, we run into problems. Rather than being able to speak more precisely about the emotion itself, usually what we will try to do is to find out what I am depressed *about*.

The problem with the way we communicate our emotions and try to delve more deeply into them, is that we tend to leave the emotion itself out. Mostly what we are doing when we are investigating an emotion is surrounding it, giving it a clearer background. That background can extend, in classical psychoanalysis, to the cradle, but as for the emotion we are experiencing itself, it can somehow not have been touched. We may both come to feel better about what we have done, but generally what will have been accomplished is a sort of dissipation and distraction.

Presumably, then, we might say that at least I myself know my emotion. But do I? If I were to describe the feeling itself to myself, what do I say? Much the same sort of thing. I am depressed about . . . death, say, separation, isolation. But these, again, are *conditions* of the emotion, frames, even causes; the emotion itself will often remain vague, uncertain, and transitory. Often it seems that by the time we are into the investigation of an emotion, that emotion has been frustratingly replaced by the one attached to the investigation. If we push ourselves to ask, What am I *really* feeling? we will probably begin to refer to the body. We will say, I am feeling this in my gut, or in my heart, or in my genitals. But this, too, tends to be rather crude. We feel, in our culture, fear in the pit of the stomach, but we also feel some components of "truth" there, and of true love.

And yet, with all of this apparent imprecision and reflective uncertainty, we know that when we are feeling something it is anything but crude, vague, and approximate. We know that we are feeling this *exact* feeling at this exact time; we know we will never feel this precise feeling again, and what's more we know exactly to what degree we are suffering from or exalting in this specific emotion. The problem seems to arise when we have to describe ourselves to ourselves. For whatever reason, human consciousness is not satisfied with experience in itself, it is our reflection on our experience that allows us to consider ourselves legitimated, that makes us recognize an emotion as authentic. Unless we can manage to accomplish this reflection, we feel we have been cheated and, in a radical sense, may even begin to question the reality of what we have experienced. Emotion, then, clearly must be considered in relation to the larger concepts of consciousness and of mind.

I'd like now to try to offer a brief characterization of mind and consciousness as I experience them myself. I don't in any sense mean to revise existing psychologies or epistemologies, and I surely don't mean to assume to tell you anything you don't already know. What I'm proposing, I think, are questions of emphasis that interest me.

The mind I experience myself seems to be a much more chaotic and turbulent phenomenon than those I've heard about: there is much more happening in it, much more happening at once, and much more happening in a nondetermined way. If I were to try to make a rough section of it, I would find first of all sense data, arriving from various parts of the body, usually through the eyes and ears, bringing with them what philosophy traditionally calls "impressions." Then there are the processing systems of these impressions, which discard most of them, filing some for future reference, although not necessarily the ones one would think to have selected. Then there are the various, and much more numerous, elements of consciousness that mind itself generates. Of these elements, what I'll discuss first, because I think it is not only the most basic of the mind's activities but the least remarked, is what I'll call the image-making mechanism. This is a phenomenon hinted at but not really captured by the term *stream of consciousness.* It is also the source of our access to "primary process," but differs from it in some essential ways.

Briefly, it is my observation that one of the major activities of the mind is the constant, incessant, and terrifically rapid production of image. I mean by image those mental pictures that exist aside from, or rather along with, but as it were *behind,* the images received by sense. There is a kind of perception screen through which we process images that arrive from the world, and a screen behind it onto which the interior images are being projected. We are always aware of which is the "real" image, but at the same time we are also always able, when we wish, to refer to the other image mechanism as it works, or plays. I have no idea how to measure the number of images that pass out of our interior world into this portion of consciousness. When I've discussed the question with young poets in my workshops, I've mentioned at least several per second, and none of my students have found that unreasonable. These images, as I say, are rapid, incessant, irrepressible (although we do learn not to pay attention to them), often utterly unreasonable in origin, and very often have nothing to do with what is going on in the rest of consciousness, with the projects of our "reality." Sometimes the images arise from memory, places seen, people known; sometimes they will have to do with words that are going through our mind at the moment. Although sometimes these images are surely the result of the action and interaction of instinctual forces, sometimes they will have no discernible genealogy, no roots whatever in anything we can account for. Sometimes the images will begin to link together—by sometimes I mean several times a minute, at least—and sometimes these linkages, fragments of narrative, will catch the attention of other portions of mind and the narratives will extend and become what we call fantasy.

It is this constant flow of image and narrative, *generated* by consciousness in a nondetermined way, that is the key, I feel, to our beginning to adequately characterize emotion. I say "characterize" purposefully, and not "embody," because the other element of my thesis is that in fact it is already embodied, with great precision and rigor, in poetry.

I'll come back to that; for now I want to continue with the scheme I'm developing, the next element of which would be language. Language is layered over and somehow weaves in and out of the flow of image and narrative-fantasy. Usually it seems to exist apart from them, but at the same time is constantly referring to the image world, recuperating portions of it for its own use, and feeding back into the image world material that would not otherwise be there. Language, of course, is an enormously complex phenomenon in itself. We know amazingly little about it; we aren't even sure whether we teach ourselves to learn language or whether, figuratively at least, it teaches us to learn it.

The way we generally experience language in consciousness is of itself of interest in terms of our emotional life. Language seems to come to us through what we might call the voice of the mind. There is a voice within us, certainly. Sometimes we hear it rather vaguely, sometimes surprisingly sharply. Sometimes it seems to speak to and for our conceived identity, sometimes it dialogues with that identity, and sometimes it is sharply critical. Usually it speaks in our everyday voice, but sometimes we can be surprised to hear someone else's voice within us. Sometimes it seems to be telling us what we had in mind to say but didn't know how to say; sometimes it refuses us utterly, denying us what we know is "on the tip of the tongue." When it speaks out into the world, it sometimes does so with our concurrence, satisfying our premeditations, but sometimes it can seem to have a perversely contradictory program of its own, hardly consulting with us, producing one of the more interesting of the mind-body syndromes: "the foot in the mouth."

Language and the voice of mind are deeply involved in, but don't entirely determine, what we call "sentiments," that is, our feeling about the general tone of the proceedings, short-term and long, in consciousness and in the world. Out of these sentiments arise our grander notions of morality, ethics, our social and political beliefs and attitudes.

And beyond all this, there is what we call thought, what is known as discursive thinking, something presumably similar to what I am attempting here. In this activity, the mind picks its way through all the littered landscapes I've been describing, making what we call rational sense, acting as though all of these detourings and blind alleys didn't exist.

The capacity of consciousness to juggle these elements of itself is, one might say, mind-boggling. What I want to emphasize most sharply in the characterization I'm offering, though, are what I've referred to as the nondetermined, apparently arbitrary phenomena generated by mind, both by way of image and language, for I feel that these arbitrary aspects of mind are in fact at the foundation of imagination. I seem to be coming into conflict here with the whole universe of psychology, particularly Freudian psychology. As we know, part of Freud's genius was to dissect, as it were, the soul into its historical components, showing how these small histories determine us. Freud's theoretical models were of course necessarily of his time. He proposed a sort of geology of consciousness that, as has been remarked, was similar to the earth science that had been elaborated in the nineteenth century, and he also proposed a vision of consciousness that we might say was Darwinian. More than that, though, the universe in which Freud situated mind was a Newtonian universe, where phenomena could be accounted for with calculus and, by extension, in a cause-and-effect relationship, however complicated this relationship would have to be. The products of consciousness itself, fantasy and dream primarily, were, for Freud, the products of tensions in the past, presumably repressed tensions. Consciousness could be accounted for, and possibly redeemed, by a scrupulous attention to these pastnesses, and part of that scrupulousness was the proposition that nothing in consciousness was arbitrary, that the mind had a Newtonian coherence.

The universe in which we find our models is quite different. It is the universe of quanta, of events that bear a quality in themselves of a kind of indeterminateness. The curves of experience our physics deals with are larger, and are describable only by attention to their larger activities. Necessity becomes statistical rather than calculable, and the possibly arbitrary nature of the individual event becomes something that must be taken into account.

The events of consciousness that I am describing seem to me to partake of a universe of possibility in which the arbitrary, the unpredictable, undetermined event has a remarkable metaphoric similarity to that of a quantum. I believe that in order for us to make our consciousnesses appear to be the neat Freudian, Newtonian mechanisms we have conceived them to be, we must do a remarkable amount of disattending, disregarding, something like what the word *repression* indicates, but probably something that is in some ways more radical.

Simultaneity is a thorny problem in epistemology, but I hold that there is something in the potential of our mind that can and does as a matter of course entertain simultaneously a startling range of content. As I was composing the sentence I am starting to say to you now, for instance—it was written in my mind late at night in bed a month or so ago in Paris—I was also thinking about what this room would look like today, what you would look like before me, of what my friend Loren would look like as he sat among you listening, of what he would think of all this, of Loren's new house, of the evening I spent there with my wife, then of a street somewhere in Italy, which came to me I had no idea why, then of another friend, then another landscape, totally unknown to me; there were also the words more or less as they are of this sentence, plus my remarking to myself how remarkable what I was doing really was; beyond all that I was humming under my breath a Robert Burns song I'd been memorizing the day before, "For A' That and A' That" (I commend it to you), and of course I was paying enough attention to all this to be able to report it, at the same time being aware that a number of images and bits of narrative had occurred to which I was too preoccupied to attend.

My point here is that I don't feel that this was an unusual moment of consciousness, at least in its complexity. Clearly we don't generally pay such meticulous attention to ourselves for very long, we wouldn't be able to go on with the business of living. We learn, as I say, to disregard most of these obscure goings-on, and it might be a measure of what we call sanity as to how successful we are at it.

I'm sure this has all seemed a very crude, oversimplified depiction of consciousness; I imagine I've omitted much I would find on further reflection even in my own mind, but I think I have given some notion of what we must take into account when we speak of something as complex and crucial to us as emotion. An emotion clearly is in direct relation to all of the elements of mind I have been discussing. Whatever the experience the emotion arises from, the mind will have to process it. During this processing, there will also be images generated into consciousness, some dictated by the experience itself, some with very little or nothing to do with it. There will also be the participation of the senses, of language as it comments, criticizes, reflects, plus there will be an awareness that the equation that all of this makes, the emotion, is something that is not a normal moment of passing consciousness. In our everyday experience, all of this will be dealt with by the mind's various components, including that one which we call "self," a sort of majority vote will be taken and the experience will then be denoted with one of the names for feeling we've received and learned to apply. Once so named, the feeling will generate another series of phenomena of its own, as well as interpretations of *these* events that will be in turn voted on, and possibly named again. There will also be a sort of checking-in process between votes to keep the mind up on what is happening on the longer term.

We can certainly say that an emotion is not a simply thing. And yet, it is the odd conceit of our culture that an emotion is the only thing in our mental lives we don't have to doubt. We are taught that there is within us something uncontaminated, pure, and which is to be the base to which all the rest of our confusing existence is to refer: our feelings. We are somehow given to assume, even more strangely, that emotions are the one thing for which we don't have to be educated. Even in the various psychotherapy systems, there seems often to be the assumption that one is to get back, somehow, through all the storm and *dreck* of the rest of mind to these islands of purity, spontaneity, and clarity.

Emotions, I hold, are in and of themselves neither pure, spontaneous, nor very clear. They require a stringent attentiveness, and, if the soul is to do justice to their turbulence and furor without belittling itself, it must indeed be educated, and rigorously so. It is my thesis that the most useful method we have devised for that education is poetry.

A poem is a wonderfully complicated instrument. It is as complicated, maybe more so, than an emotion. It also shares many characteristics with emotion. It is composed of sensation, of image, language, a voice, perception, bodily reference, sentiment, morality, thought, and experience. It, like existence itself, concerns itself crucially with the arbitrary and the determined. The forms of poetry, for instance, are in a large sense totally arbitrary. What we call a convention is a system of the arbitrary and the necessary. That the most common rhythmic convention in English poetic history, iambic pentameter, has ten syllables, five stressed and five unstressed, is determined to some extent by the nature of the language itself, but in another sense it has nothing to do with it. The line might have easily had six feet, or been syllabically determined. The fact that the line—and the other conventions of poetry—are arbitrarily determined is of the utmost importance, because it is in the tension between the artificially determined conventions and the necessities of language and experience that the music of poetry arises, and the music of poetry, that is of consciousness at play in the fields of necessity and crisis, is one of the most important informing elements of poetry. So, too, do what we call figuration, simile, metaphor, and so forth have to do with the arbitrary and the necessary. We are taught that it is associative necessity that determines metaphor, but this is not the case. It is actually the ability of the poet to *dissociate,* to reach into the realm of chance, to fuse the unlikely with the undeniable, that determines the intensity of metaphor. So, the German poet Rilke, for instance, in contemplating the tombs of ancient Roman courtesans, trying to find their imaginative identity, ends up comparing the women, to, of all unlikely things, rivers, "and," he says,

> over them in brief, impetuous waves
> (each wanting to prolong itself, forever)
> the bodies of countless adolescents surged;
> and in them roared the currents of grown men.
> And sometimes boys would burst forth from the mountains
> of childhood, and would descend in timid streams
> and play with what they found on the river's bottom,
> until the steep slope gripped their consciousness.

The tensions of poetry are, of course, most evident and most crucial in their direct relation to experience. Poetry deals with the most difficult of our experiences and emotions, and these dealings are dictated by the sharpest necessities. Poetry confronts in the most clear-eyed way just those emotions that consciousness most wishes to slide by, and it deals with them in their greatest profundity, with the most refined moral sensibility, and what's more it does justice to just the sorts of complexities and simultaneities I have been sketching here.

At the beginning of this talk, I proposed a situation in which I would say to you, "I am depressed," and I tried to point out how vague and uncertain this statement really is, whether spoken to others or to the self. I hinted that my depression had to do with death, separation, isolation. What I would like to do now is to offer you two poems, both by Emily

Dickinson, both having to do with depression, and with death. Each incorporates a specific emotion, elaborates it, analyzes it, and, in a deep sense, redeems it. For poetry ultimately has to do most of all with that, with the redemption of our experiences from the temporal and the trivial.

The first poem is *about* depression. It is the most complete depiction and embodiment of depression I know, of the actual *emotion* of depression, the emotion that I pointed out, in our normal experience is surrounded, backgrounded, but rarely articulated directly. Dickinson in this poem uses the imagery of death, figures of death, actual apprehensions of death, to work with the emotion. She never tells us what her depression is "about"; perhaps that would be a trivialization of it. Here is the poem.

> I felt a Funeral, in my Brain,
> And Mourners to and fro
> Kept treading—treading—till it seemed
> That Sense was breaking through—
>
> And when they all were seated,
> A Service, like a Drum—
> Kept beating—beating—till I thought
> My Mind was going numb—
>
> And then I heard them lift a Box
> And creak across my Soul
> With those same Boots of Lead, again,
> Then Space—began to toll,
>
> As all the Heavens were a Bell,
> And Being, but an Ear,
> And I, and Silence, some strange Race
> Wrecked, solitary, here—
>
> And then a Plank in Reason, broke,
> And I dropped down, and down—
> And hit a World, at every plunge,
> And Finished knowing—then—

What it is that Dickinson knows, and finishes knowing, at the end of the poem is almost too frightening to consider. She has confronted, in her investigation of that single emotion, the annihilation of consciousness, the loss of reason in its harrowing proximities to nothingness. She has enacted the terrifying closed system of depression, in which content, sense, reality all became function of that closure. The images that occur, once the system has been impelled, after the vehicle of the funeral has been established, still partake of the kind of arbitrary mental event that I tried to sketch before, but their apparent arbitrariness only contributes to the tensions and despair of the mental experience. A "Service, like a Drum": there is no drum in the funerals of life, only in the rituals of depression, in which the heart itself seems to become the enemy of the organism and of consciousness. The "Boots of Lead" are heavier and more excruciating than any we know. The "Heavens" that become a bell: all of infinite space emptied of its possible divinities, of its potential solace, so that all of Being, all the being of the individual and all the creatures of existence can do nothing but listen to that divine space, now encapsulated and captured in the bell of skull, and of emotion. And the plank: is it the plank that a pirate's victim must walk, or a plank covering a dry well, the well of inexistence? The ambiguities are as crucial as the precisions: the layering of meaning and potential meaning in the poem are the very layers of consciousness. That this dire experience could be put into words, that the voice of the mind could make it cohere, that the language of the experience could, what's more, be organized into rhythm patterns, that there could even be rhyme, all the while upholding the dark integrities of the experience itself: this is not the product of mind, this *is* mind, and emotion, and the human soul alive to itself.

The other poem is very similar in some ways. It is a poem that occupies itself with death, but this time death is not being used to incorporate another emotion, rather it is death itself that is being confronted, our fear of death, our apprehensions at how the mind deals and will deal with death. You'll notice that the poem works again by using imagery and sensations that surround the experience of human dying, but in this case the theme of the poem is the subtraction of the imagery of the soul by death. Note that the poem is in the past tense, although clearly the events it speculates are in an imagined future. At the same time, our reading of the poem must take place in a narrative present. Hence, even as the poem launches itself we are in a mind-situation of complexity and tension.

> I heard a Fly buzz—when I died—
> The Stillness in the Room
> Was like the Stillness in the Air—
> Between the Heaves of Storm—
>
> The Eyes around—had wrung them dry—
> And Breaths were gathering firm
> For that last Onset—when the King
> Be witnessed—in the Room—
>
> I willed my Keepsakes—Signed away
> What portion of me be
> Assignable—and then it was
> There interposed a Fly—
>
> With Blue—uncertain stumbling Buzz—
> Between the light—and me—
> And then the Windows failed—and then
> I could not see to see—

Someone is dying, a someone who is called "I," a name with which we all are familiar. The room the "I" is in is quiet, so quiet that a single fly can be heard, but the quiet is ominous, it promises to give way to great violence, as of a storm, a violence that of course finally occurs in a stillness yet deeper. The "I" of the poem is surrounded by other people, who have cried and who now, in the face of the enormities of death, can do nothing but wait. The one who is dying speaks her testament, and then the fly is there. Suddenly we realize that everything in the room has become the fearful function now of mind itself. The other human beings become equal to the fly, then the fly becomes equal to the dying self, and to light itself, and to existence itself.

"And then the Windows failed—and then / I could not see to see—." The loss of actual subjecthood has been imagined, apprehended, and redeemed. The poem struggles with resignation, with all the resignations we try to teach ourselves, and it accomplishes these resignations with wisdom and grace. I "Signed away / What portion of me be / Assignable." The portion of me that had to do with you, with us, with all of us, all the other subjects that are our consolation, but a consolation that no longer will operate, that we must renounce. And then this wise renunciation itself has no more reality than the fly, which still intrudes, insists, equating our time with its, and then the fly, the tiny morsel of eternity, is gone, and then the light in which it swam is gone, "the Windows failed." The windows of sense, of soul, of self, of subject, but, too, the windows even of our attempt to contemplate the unendurable fact of death. Only the voice is left now, only the voice of mind, as it enacts, no longer with horror, no longer with fear, because there is nothing left to be horrified or fearful with, the going out of not only sight but of the sight behind sight, the very vision of the mind and soul. When the poem ends, when that voice stops, the silence that falls upon us is the silence of death and inexistence.

It is thus that poetry speaks its emotion, its consciousness. It is thus that it teaches us the limits of the elements of consciousness we value so—our reason, our discursive language, our notion that we can analyze the substances of being. Perhaps the real matter of the human soul is poetry itself; perhaps it is in the community that is established between the speaking soul of the poet and the attending soul of the listener that our consciousness, our culture and our selves find their ways of being saved from the awful deaths we imagine and die, the awful ephemeralities of our passage through eternity, and the awful disattendings to what we have of that passage.

The Poet and History

We too had many pretty toys when young:
A law indifferent to blame or praise,
To bribe or threat; habits that made old wrong
Melt down, as it were wax in the sun's rays. . . .

1

For a long time I have deeply envied the great poems of Yeats's middle period, the long poems of *The Tower,* in particular, "Nineteen Hundred and Nineteen," "Meditations in Time of Civil War," and "The Tower," but recently I've come to realize that my feelings go beyond the poet's normal admiration of excellence and genius. What I have been jealous of is the way that Yeats's poetic prime and the moment during his life of the most intense historical necessity had coincided so sharply. Never mind that the poems are works of great sadness, nearly cries of anguish, for the Europe that was devouring itself in the nationalism of the Great War, and for his adored Ireland tearing itself to pieces for ideals as ill grounded and as misbegotten, and for which Yeats felt, and may even have borne, some responsibility: "And I myself created Hanrahan / And drove him drunk or sober through the dawn / From somewhere in the neighboring cottages." Yeats was fifty-four in 1919, at the peak of his poetic power. The rest of his poetic life would be wonderfully fertile, in some ways he would become an even more interesting

© C. K. Williams. Delivered as a talk on January 5, 1985, to the M.F.A. students at Warren Wilson College. First published in *TriQuarterly,* 1988.

poet later on, but never would there be works that had such a broad resonance, such a brilliant fusing of the personal and public, the individual and the general, the autobiographical and the historical. The person Yeats was and the poet he had made of himself as an actor in history came together in a poetry whose very music arose out of the conflicts of his awareness of that history and whose very beauty was soaked in horror, like the mother in "Nineteen Hundred and Nineteen," who must "crawl in her own blood."

It is quite feasible and not at all aesthetically immoral to define poetry in such a way that one has to feel neither a particular responsibility toward history nor any squeamishness about apparently omitting such concerns from one's work. The traditions of poetry are rooted as much in pure song, "life's own self-delight," to quote Yeats again, as they are in any sort of "meaning," whether historical, political, philosophical, or otherwise. A poem is grounded in its time, whether it articulates its consciousness of this or not, and it does not have to manifest a direct awareness of its historical situation in order to be significant and to fulfill a rich definition of poetry.

At the same time, once one does decide to try for whatever personal reasons to commit one's poetry as intentionally as possible to questions of direct historical and social significance, issues are raised that are not easily evaded, the central one of which seems to me to be this: how am I to reconcile my sense of limitation, even of inadequacy, in terms of my own actual position in history, with the apparently heroic self which these sorts of meditation seem to call for? If, as Wittgenstein could say, "The World is the case," how is one, as it were, really to take oneself as the lyric case?

2

The most extreme, and the most heroic, example we have in literature of the poet indeed taking himself as the case is Dante. Dante's entire comedy was as profoundly immersed in his vision of history as it was in his vision of the divine, and much of his greatness is in his fusion of realms, his bringing human history and divine history into congruence: the moral and the pragmatic, the metaphysical and the autobiographical.

Dante's technique for enacting these unifications was to designate himself as humanity's visionary, as the sole living human being who would be allowed, through the power of the inspiration of his mortal love for Beatrice, to explore the realms of the dead and of the eternal afterlife. Dante was to be the spiritual hero of the entire human adventure: it was he, and we only through him, who would actually experience how humans in history find their ultimate rewards and punishment in divine judgment. Dante is historically very specific: there are those he wishes to praise, and those he will blame—indeed, damn. There are popes whose actions he will find reprehensible, and kings like Charles Martel he will consider as lost saviors of the divine-human potential. Dante set the time of his travel through afterlife a dozen or so years before he was actually working on his poem so that he would be not only a moral mediator but an accurate prophet of what he found the limiting and destructive tendencies of his contemporaries. The history about which Dante was writing, and which fired so many of his deepest feelings, was a history that begins and ends in eternity but is enacted in an absolute present as banal and immediate as our own relentless quotidian. Those who carry out Dante's dramas of redemption are his acquaintances—indeed, his neighbors—as well as the princes and petty kings of Italy. Dante was to be the hero of the human attempt, but he was to be at the same time the flesh-and-blood Dante who was insecure enough in his human condition to need a mentor, a guide, a hero of his own, to take him through the more dire portions of his journey.

The reality of Dante's character, and the feelings of self-worthlessness he experiences, is one of the recurring themes of the work. Dante is continually breaking down, swooning, swearing that he can no longer go on: first Virgil, then Beatrice have to hearten him, reassure him, sometimes chastise him for his timorousness and uncertainty. In the *Purgatorio* and *Paradiso,* this fear gradually becomes interwoven with the virtue of humility, so absolutely essential to the Christian soul, and in the glorious redemptive vision Dante experiences in paradise, even this self-doubt is accounted for.

In the *Inferno,* though, where the non-Christian Virgil is

Dante's teacher, the issue is quite different. Again, our casual response to Virgil's function in the *Commedia* has to do with his direct knowledge of limbo and of hell and purgatory: he is to instruct Dante, to encourage him past the frightful examples of human fallibility and evil before which Dante will quail. I believe, though, that Virgil's actual function is more elemental and much more basic: it is to enable Dante to make that leap by which he will in fact take himself as the case, in which he will dare to assume for himself the poet, and for poetry, tasks which were hitherto only incidentally conceived of as a part of their definitions. What Dante needed from Virgil was the model of someone who had dared himself to try to recapitulate various modes of history, however much Virgil's experience was limited from a Christian point of view.

The unification of apparently contradictory historical systems is actually one of the oldest gestures of significant literature: it begins for us with Homer's warriors, who inhabit a half-mythic world of gods and absolute passions, and Aeschylus's Orestes, who flees from mythic history to the symbolic reality of Athens. When we participate in literature as readers, we are so accustomed to this movement that we hardly remark it, so deftly does Milton, as another example, poeticize his metaphysic and embody his historical-ethical imperatives in the divine history he is reincarnating. But when we, as poets, consider that movement, that attempt, that task, it is a forbidding undertaking. There are presumptions, about the self, about the social, about the metaphysical, so gigantic that one does not, literally, know how to begin: the sheer *will*, the intensity of the overcoming of one's vision of self that is called for, is so daunting.

Naturally we don't believe that we can will ourselves to be Dantes or Miltons, and neither do we—or most of us, anyway— have such a clear vision of the varieties of divine and human history: even if we are deeply religious, there has been in the conceptual mind of the West an apparently quite irrevocable split between the workings-out of the secular and the holy.

At the same time, though, history, past and future, remains for us the necessary matrix in which our most profound ideas and ideals will be enacted. Our metaphysics and our ethic evolve in a dialectic with whatever spiritual structure we happen to be born into or to construct for ourselves; but without the connection to a concrete historical reality with its necessities and its responsibilities and demands, we cannot even refer to an ethic as such: it will be simply a sort of Boy Scout handbook to good deeds.

It is here that our presumption isn't so audacious in defining ourselves by a spiritual gesture similar to the heroic Dante's, for we, too, when we dare to try to conceive of ourselves as active agents, active participants in the larger social and political histories around us, experience an acute and painful sense of insignificance and uncertainty. The actual history Dante participated in, the ebb and flow of those human events he could quite clearly visualize as beginning at least as far back as the early Roman Empire and culminating in the Guelph-Ghibelline dispute, was quite accessible to him—perhaps in his exile he may even have thought it too much so. But where is our history now, how do we dare to think that we are actually participating in it in an ethically direct way, rather than being more observers of it, passive recipients?

There is serious debate about whether the individual's actual experience of self in history has really been heightened since the age of revolutions, since our rights as democratic agents have been elaborated for us, or whether many of us have not in fact become more separated from a real sense of a position in a history that is supposed to include us directly as a part of its purposes. Whether because of the difficult disjunctions of industrialism, or the developments of bureaucratic governments that have in mind their own interests and perpetuation before anything else, it is really quite feasible for us to say that in many ways we are actually more estranged from a history that would be intimately available to us as individuals, than was the situation in the days when our situations were certainly more humble but more clearly defined.

I do not in any way mean to suggest here any sort of reaction or reversion to a condition that in nearly every other sense was intolerable: what I am indicating is that in some ways the courage that is demanded of us, the difficulties that face us in joining our intimate biographies to humanity's, are even greater, and possibly demand a heroism more rigorous than Dante's or Milton's.

Frank O'Connor, in *The Lonely Voice,* defines the short story as different from the novel not so much by its length or for any technical reason but because, instead of having a hero, it has what he calls a "submerged population group" which may be, he points out, "Gogol's officials, Turgenev's serfs, Maupassant's prostitutes, Chekhov's doctors and teachers, Sherwood Anderson's provincials." O'Connor's arguments are compelling, but what is most interesting here is the term "submerged population," because I think that quite possibly it is not merely the short story that can be defined by the phrase but the consciousness of nearly all human beings in modern civilization.

How many American writers can one name, at least since 1850, who have *not* felt themselves to have risen out of some marginal group or submerged social class? How many of us can *assume* an involvement in history that has anything more than that observer status I alluded to? Among poets, there would be only Lowell, I think. Lowell was obsessed by history, and a good part of his obsession seemed to find its roots in his family genealogy, the power and status of the Boston Lowells in American history. Lowell is aware of himself as at least potentially a patrician, the heir of a living body of events that were his by blood, as much as by concept. But when you go to his brilliant poems of history, they are in all but a few instances scholar's poems, the poems of the well-read dilettante. In the few poems in which Lowell does actually himself enter into the stream of living events, in his acquaintances with Robert Kennedy and Gene McCarthy, in his participation in the Pentagon march of the 1960s, his sense of being out of place, a usurper, a pretender, is as acute as that of Norman Mailer's, although Mailer could idealize Lowell as the living embodiment of various unattainable patrimonies and sureties Mailer felt were forbidden to him.

The sense of being outside of things is not an American phenomenon of course: from Baudelaire to Vallejo, the poet's image of being at the margins of society: sending poems toward a center, has been almost the primary description of the poet's situation, or plight.

So there seems to be a double overcoming demanded of the modern poet who would take upon himself or herself the business of history, of being in history, or responsibility toward it and of conscious enactment in it. Not only is one presuming mightily to take oneself as the case, but even the larger group to which one belongs seems invariably to have a tangential relation to the direct realm of politics and social choice, to that world which one hopes is to be affected by the labors of the poet and the poem.

To observe, to comment, to pass notes back and forth to one another is not to participate in history as Dante or Yeats did. How are we to find our way, then, to a place near enough to the center so that our efforts to affect that center are not so feeble and futile that there is no point in even beginning, even putting pen to paper?

3

A year or so ago, in an undergraduate creative-writing class, we were discussing nuclear war. It was the week of the showing of what turned out to be that lame film *The Day After,* and we had quite a lively discussion going. At one point, one of my more articulate students said something that at the time I more or less dismissed but that I've thought of often since. What he said in essence was: "Why worry so much about all of this? If there's going to be a nuclear war, there'll be one; it won't be for us to decide. Why pretend that we have anything to do with the choice? Why should we shorten our lives with worry?" (One of my other students chipped in that he'd heard the whole nuclear-freeze debate was a result of manipulation by the Russians, who were trying to shorten American life-expectancy by inducing stress in us.)

As I say, at first I didn't think much of what my good student had offered: I suppose I gave him some homilies about participatory democracy and the like, but, after I'd thought about it for a while, I came to realize that what he'd been making wasn't a polemic but a plea. Not to me, not to anyone in particular, but to things as they are, to reality itself. What he was asking, I think, was that he be allowed to live a while longer in his child's mind, that mind we begin with and which we carry with us all our lives that tells us that the adults are somehow, we don't know and we don't care how, going to take care of this, of anything and everything. The child broods and frets about ultimate issues much more than we give it credit for—anyone who has ever had a child recovering from even minor illness knows this—but those worries almost always subside into the conviction that those who are responsible for us will deal with what troubles us. And usually, of course, they do: most of us do have our bread on the table; we do have our beds to sleep in.

The hardest part about becoming adults is in giving up this conviction, in having to take responsibility for our own acts and actions, even, finally, for the well-being of our own children. But there is something in us that always longs to return to that past time of warmth and protectedness. Much of the working-out of our characters, we might even say, is a drama between those two tendencies in our psyches, and I think we could also describe our societal life, as well, as the conflict between the movement toward autonomy and the inertias of dependence that the child manifests.

Democratic government, for instance, in America at least, has come almost to rely on a general passivity and immobility on the part of the populace, except during elections, when presumably our affectedness is to be expressed and our general will enacted. Any sort of stirring of the waters between these carefully scheduled times, anything beyond letter-writing to congressmen and allowing one's pulse to be taken in polls, government tends to find subversive, and, if expressing disagreement, even dangerous: in the socialist world, such dissent is considered outright treason. Government, then, would have us understand and accept that we are, in fact, children, that *it* is the adult, and that when we trouble it with our little wants—about nuclear war, for instance—all we're doing is intruding, impeding government from getting on with its business of taking care of us.

It isn't by chance that I use nuclear war as an instance here. I believe that the threat of nuclear war and of ecological apocalypse, including the population explosion, are much more central to our considerations of identity and of self than is usually given credence. I believe that the reality we all live in now has demanded of us a terrific act of repression of both the individual and collective psyche. I think that every morning when we awake and don't cry out in terror at the vile extinction that looms above us, we are reflexively defending ourselves with walls of psychic numbness as real and as debilitating as any neurosis. We can, and perhaps must, accept this mode of conscious life as necessary, as inescapable, and if we envisage nuclear holocaust or the extinction of the planet as just so many individual deaths, then perhaps that is the case: we are all simply making the ancient gesture by which we protect ourselves against a too-vivid awareness of our mortality.

But I think the issues are more insidious than that. What we face in our age is not the death of so many individuals, but the death of the species itself, and this sort of total collective perishing is of a different quality entirely from individual death. The animal, and the human being, will under many circumstances sacrifice its individual life to the good of the species, to what we call the common good but which we might better understand as the historic good: the good by which the specie-body and the specie-identity will survive the individual. I think that when we are threatened by the death of all of us at once, of the species, there may very well be something in our genetic structure itself that makes our very organism cry out to us to act to avert this encompassing disaster. And perhaps we have another anguish: perhaps we know that what we fear comes from our realization that human existence is in some intimate connection to something greater than itself, and our deeper sadness might have as much to do with images of consciousness itself bringing itself to naught; it is the potential sadness of existence itself, or of God, which tears us so, with anguish, and perhaps with a pity that utterly transcends anything else we have ever felt.

But we don't *feel* all of these things, or only occasionally: we allow them to subside into those quieter portions of the psyche where they don't impinge on our everydayness, our wish to live, to experience, to possess lives as near to "normal" as we can. But what if the despair that we imagine awaits us with the annihilations of species and of consciousness in fact informs our souls as a much more constantly compelling fact that we take into account? Might we, in other words, be living in a state of despair right now, without quite even knowing it? And, further, as poets, might not this despair be unconsciously affecting our very definition of poetry, and even the ways in which we execute it?

In the course of my teaching, and of various other literary business—judging contests, editing, trying to keep up with and to encourage hopeful young poets—I get to read a really quite astounding number of poems. I'm not going to comment on the level of competence the poems might manifest—this has become a sort of whining hobby among the literati and shows little awareness of how literary culture actually operates—but I am struck by one thing, and that is the forbidding number of poems that deal with themes of childhood, that have to do with conflicts and memories about parents, grandparents, childhood traumas, schoolfriends, and so forth. As we know, since Wordsworth (although, interestingly, rarely before, excluding Traherne) the child, the child we were, is a necessary part of any serious meditation on self and society, and since Freud the tools and techniques of these introspections have become even richer. But I have the sense that such considerations are not really at the base of quite *this* much domestic obsessiveness. Neither does it arise from the unfortunate creative-writing class dictum of "writing what we know" (an instruction, by the way, that is harder than one might think either to surmount or really to make effective).

I wonder—and I'll only offer this as speculation because it might seem so far-fetched—I wonder if what might be behind all of this is in fact the despair we do feel before our dire potential fate and the impotence that overwhelms us when we consider how little say we actually have in possibly averting that fate? I wonder if our minds, despite our best will, might reel back to what I've called the child's mind, without consulting us at all about it, without even letting us know about it. Might we actually be living in a state of psychic emergency, something equivalent to the battlefield traumas that were a part of the inspiration for Freud's elaboration of the death instinct? And might we, so traumatized, be responding with really quite paralyzing gestures of psychic self-defense?

As I say, this sounds rather far-fetched, but I think it does bear consideration, especially in the terms of any consideration of the poet and history, and of the will that is clearly necessary if we are to insert ourselves into history.

There's another thing I've noticed about the younger poets I teach and have contact with, and that is how single-minded and passionate their dedication is to becoming accomplished poets. We usually consider such commitment to an art as an admirable end to be desired, and of course it is. But there's something I sometimes find troubling about how *exclusive* this dedication can seem. It sometimes seems to entail a sort of myopia, or even tunnel vision: the poet's world becomes so absolutely focused on poetry and poets that I can have the queasy feeling that I'm dealing with people who are partly illiterate in terms of any other system of knowledge and value. Another speculation: might this potential overdedication, this narrowing of interest and of competence, of system and of existence, be also a result of the despair I've been trying to articulate? That my students know little and care little about philosophy—about history, science, anthropology, art—is this a part of the ordinary poet's madness we know is in our cultural heritage, or might this much intensity, an intensity that excludes so much, be rather something new? Might there not be a different sort of sacrifice implied than our traditional marriage to our art? Might a portion of our humanity be at risk?

I speak of the younger poets, but I have to say that these are tendencies and directions I've felt in myself as well, which is perhaps why I dare to offer such possible affront to so many I admire. I feel in myself a constant leaning toward a sort of limiting ambition, a tendency to become a poetic grind; I feel myself overwhelmed with a moral indolence about what certain tasks of my identity as human being, rather than as poet, entail.

What are those tasks? What does it mean to have an identity as a human being beyond that of the poet? We all, of course, define ourselves in many systems, and any of us would indeed be affronted to have only a single definition. Another observation, and another speculation: I have noticed also, and not only among my students now, that there is very little philosophizing these days about the nature of the human. Very rarely in our poems does one find the sorts of reflection on the basic attributes of the human soul, as, to our examples again, are in Dante, Milton, or Yeats. Possibly there is nothing to fret about here because such reflection, such philosophical work, is assumed by any literary artifact. But might the question be deeper, might it be that something keeps us from reflecting on the nature of the human as the starting point of our mature considerations?

I am going to postulate another genre of despair now, possibly more available to our consciousness than the nuclear and ecological anguish we must live with but possibly just as much an obstacle to be overcome if we are to conceive of ourselves as participants and real agents of our history.

The process of defining our humanity is always an argument between our vision of what we see before us—the evidence—and of what we can conceive ideally for the human. What we call philosophical thinking is actually much more firmly grounded in the life we live, even the life philosophers live, than philosophy itself admits. Our image of philosophical thought is of an activity purified of the mucks and manias of human interchange and human emotion, but the dialectic by which one arrives at the most abstruse notions of consciousness and of ethical purpose should and must be embedded in the realities of history as fact and history as possibility. It is between these facts and these possibilities that the dialectic of our first definitions depends, and the task we must set ourselves in trying to make ourselves conscious of our philosophical and historical situation has very much to do with trying to clarify both the terms of that dialectic and what the facts of our history actually have been.

The facts of our recent history are nearly as depressing as our nuclear future. War, oppression, colonialism, concentration camps: the human animal hangs its head in shame, but our spirits have survived all of these; we have retained our hope, or so we like to think. But have we indeed kept a hope as real and as vibrant as that which poets have traditionally assumed? If defining the human reality also entails dreaming the human possibility, where are we in our history now? André Brink succinctly sums up the results of some centuries of human attempt by saying, "We are living amid the ruins of not one, but two, utopian visions of the world." The two empires Brink refers to are of course the capitalist-Christian and the socialist-communist. Whatever one's political attitudes and ideals, it does not take a great deal of effort, if not to agree with Brink, then to entertain his point of view. Clearly capitalism as we know it is terribly flawed. The wealth and well-being it has undeniably brought to so many has also been forbidden to just as many, or more. Whether all the rich of the world are riding on the backs of the poor is a matter to be debated, but that those poor, whether in the Third World or in the slums of the industrial democracies, are not along on the rosy railroad of capitalist progress is certain. The failings of

Soviet and Eastern communism are different but equally dismal. Societies in which the expression of the individual—whether artist, writer, or union member—is deemed to be a threat to the fabric of the society, can in no sense claim the mantle of idealism that Marx postulated for them. In some ways, then, the result of all our philosophizing, all the grand and good intent of all our houses, has been so disastrous that the attempt to define ourselves with any level of conviction seems to be nullified in advance, because we know by experience how such philosophical certainties will come to be enacted: in fanaticism, distortion, and hideous violence.

4

A friend of mine—a very good novelist—and I were recently discussing the Czech writer Milan Kundera. My friend said admiringly of him, "He writes about politics without you even knowing he's doing it." I agreed with my friend, but at the same time I was puzzled: why was it that we would find so virtuous such a mode of indirection? If one wishes to talk about politics in one's work, why shouldn't one? And, in fact, Kundera in his recent work does just that, but the point I was groping toward had more to do with my friend and me than with whatever our system of valuation was that would make us think this. There are several ways to consider the question. First of all, one might say that literature by its very definition is not political, that it "transcends" politics and partisan political thinking. This is something one used to hear quite often in literature classes and literary journals, and it is to a great extent true that much literature works, to use the term again, by *assuming* the political and social reality as a background against which the rest of the work is enacted, and it presumably will illuminate that background for those who care to investigate it.

There's another wariness that we might feel beyond this, though, about this question, which has to do with wishing at all costs that our work not be considered as propaganda, in any sense of the term. To be too direct in one's expression of a political point of view is to lay one's self open to being "merely" a propagandist, a spokesman for that point of view. There is certainly enough in our recent history to make us suspicious of being front men for some party's ideological manipulations.

Both of these are feasible reasons for the indirection my friend was tacitly advocating. But might there be something else, something darker and more fearful in it? I've spoken of our nuclear despair, our philosophical despair: might there be another genre of despair, of near hopelessness that has to do with our effectiveness, our real sense of what the possibilities are for any individual, even the artist who has access to more than individual means, to do anything more than touch reality in the most oblique way? Dante wrote a treatise to advise rulers how they could govern their realms so as to best make matrices for a truly Christian empire on earth. He assumed his work would be read by the very princes he was addressing. A great part of the *Commedia,* too, is devoted to the embodiment of Dante's ideas on empire, good and bad rulers and the like, which, again, he presumed would come to the attention of those he wished to affect.

What poet among us would dare dream of such influence and such effect, of actually demanding a place in the living historical reality of our time? Would it not be the most outrageous hubris for us even to consider the possibility? But what if that hubris were not simply a condition of our existence, but rather something that arose out of a historical reality that defines our essential position for us? What if this hubris, this fear of pride, is really a fear of facing our own impotence, our lack of influence, or even our abdication from one of the rightful and primary functions of the poet and the poem?

What if, we might say, we have been *cheated* of history?

5

Poetry is power.

Perhaps it is a power that we are a little afraid of, that our situation in our social-political reality *not* as poets, but as people, has made us mistrust. We know that power in the modern world is the ability to change minds, to convince, often against the real interests of those whose desires are being manipulated, whether by advertising or by politician who are genuises of image and of shadow. That is propaganda: our best selves learn to distrust propaganda, and perhaps we begin to consider our own work as potentially what we despise. We come to believe that what tries too hard to convince is not to be trusted. Therefore, we can actually mistrust our own work, its affective capabilities, its capacity for evoking in others what we passionately and painfully feel about the world ourselves.

And besides all of this, we don't even quite know to whom we're speaking. We certainly wouldn't dream that a prince, in whatever disguise, would ever run across our work. We imagine a sort of literary bureaucracy, consisting of critics, scholars, and professors, who act as agents between the poem and its audience, a selection committee, a panel of judges: the world of poetry becomes a sort of Miss America contest.

And even if we did have a more direct access to our audience, what would that audience be, to whom would we be speaking? Isn't our basic assumption about our audience that it would rather be watching television than, at best, reading a novel? But is this really the case, or is it another instance of how our perception of our function has been distorted? One of the cardinal sins of the poet is to undervalue our audience's capacities and our own efficacies.

Whitman noted: "I saw the profoundest service that poems or any other writings can do for their reader is not merely to satisfy the intellect, or supply something polished and interesting, nor even to depict great passions, or persons or events, but to fill him with vigorous and clean manliness, religiousness, and give him *good heart* as a radical possession and habit."

A good heart. If the power of propaganda is to change minds, perhaps the power of the poem is to change the soul, because the poem is the most direct means of communication with the soul. What we call the soul is really a kind of song, a fugue of thoughts and emotions, perceptions, beliefs, ideals, hopes. It is what drives the philosophers to distraction because they are trying to isolate an entity that can be spoken of precisely and defined precisely, but the soul is too complex, and too grand, for the mind, even the philosophical mind, to grasp. Poetry speaks incidentally *of* the soul, but it is the most articulate language we have for speaking directly *to* the soul.

But of what are we to speak?

In the song of the soul, everything is fused and balanced: all that we value, all that we conceive, is somehow elaborated into an order the harmonious working of which is the most profound delight of our existence. In that song, that hymn, our metaphysics marry with our morals, our ethics interweave with our notions of personal identity, our ideas of love are inextricably bound into our religious beliefs. Dante's work is the great expression of this song and of the unity we possess, but the world has changed since Dante, history has changed, what we conceive the greater world to be has changed, and even the function and use of poetry has changed.

In the modern world, the world since Baudelaire at least, and possibly the world since Blake, the peculiar function of poetry is that it is always the first element of our existence that expresses the disorder of our soul's song, that enacts the breaking down of modes of harmony between the private and the public, between the individual and the common. It is not infeasible for us to imagine ourselves as being as whole as anyone in Dante's age, but the preliminary labors toward that wholeness seem much more complex now. Which is what these reflections have really been about. Because the task of inserting ourselves as poets into history is not something that happens in the public world, in our lives as citizens, but in our monologues as selves. It is the most intimate activity for the poet; it is one of the most basic demands in the life of the poet.

We are in history, like it or not. The only question is how conscious we will be of how history is affecting us, and how we are possibly to affect it. Dante's history, too, afflicted him with despair and hopelessness. Yeats's "Nineteen Hundred and Nineteen" is a cry of anguish at the pass to which humanity seems to have brought itself. There must be a place within our poetry, too, for such naked cries of indignation and terror, of truth and of lost truth, even if the final truth seems—we hope it only seems—to be that we are helpless and that it would be terrifyingly easy to regard the human adventure as brutal and hideous.

The grounds for our despair are compelling, our sense of impotence and hopelessness insidious and debilitating. But what is asked of us then is a greater consciousness of our plight, for human history *is*, finally, consciousness; it is the ground for our experience and our despair, but it is also the recognition of our triumphs over that despair. What our poetry cannot allow itself is a perfunctory acceptance of experience as it is received, however elegantly that experience can be expressed, for this is to slight both history and ourselves, the selves we are and the selves we might become, both as individuals and as nations, peoples and humanity.

On Heine

Imagine a poet with the lyrical delicacy of Campion, the self-dramatizing flair of Byron (he called himself the German Byron), the wit of Burns, the satirical ferocity of Swift; a poet who also wrote prose like a more political Sterne, with that much verve, that much hilariously digressive amplitude, wrote enormous quantities of it, on every subject, from politics to art to philosophy and religion to folk traditions, revolutionizing prose-writing in his language while he was at it; a poet who lived through one of the most turbulent and fascinating periods of Western history—and you will have Harry Heine, the son of a failed businessman, born in Düsseldorf in 1797, who died Heinrich Heine, a famous poet and social critic, in Paris in 1856, admired, and sometimes despised, in all the countries of Europe. (And in the Americas as well: the first edition of his complete works was a pirated version published in Philadelphia.)

Now take that enormous, seemingly undeniable figure and blur him, almost erase him; make his poetry untranslatable, at least in the dominant poetic modes of our time (imagine a poet with the visionary scope of Whitman writing in the meters of Poe); and make a good portion of his prose seem dated, almost quaint. Heine's primary analytical and polemical tools were irony and satire, which are so intricately woven into the particulars of their occasion that they often don't age very well, and lose the edge of their indignation, the pressures of their conviction. His poetry untuned, his prose distempered, what happens

Review of *The Poet Dying: Heinrich Heine's Last Years in Paris* by Ernst Pawel. © C. K. Williams. First published in *The New Republic,* November 6, 1995.

to Heine? Do we lose him, and condemn him to a footnoted life in comp lit?

The late Ernst Pawel had the felicitous notion of using the story of Heine's grueling and noble death to resurrect him for us. Pawel also provides a concise recreation of his social and political moment, and he restores Heine as the powerful cultural protagonist he was considered to be in his own time. And although he never quite says so, Pawel, who wrote a celebrated study of Kafka called *The Nightmare of Reason,* also wants to make of Heine one of those heroes, like Kafka, who are an essential element of our intellectual identity.

Even for an experienced biographer like Pawel, this is not an easy endeavor. For one thing, there's the problem of Heine's poetry in English. Listen to Schubert's setting of Heine's little poem "The Doppelgänger" in the *Schwanengesang* cycle, and you will hear a passionate, tempestuous love story charged with a rich and convincing pathos, a miniature three-act tragedy. Then read the version by Hal Draper, whose dutiful translation of the complete poems has become the standard version in English, and you will hear something else:

> The night is still, the streets are dumb,
> This is the house where dwelt my dear;
> Long since she's left the city's hum
> But the house stands in the same place here.

This is the first stanza. And it could have been worse. A passage from a recent translation reads:

> When of a morning early
> I happen to pass your place,
> I am happy to see you, dear girlie,
> Stand at the window case.

But we shouldn't entirely blame the translators. The reasons a poet can't be brought across a language barrier have to do with larger matters of literary tradition and taste. (Witness Nabokov's ill-fated effort to do Pushkin in English; despite the former's assurances to the contrary, the latter's genius remains as obscure to the American reader as ever.) Given the musical norms of contemporary American poetry, there's probably no way to make more than barely acceptable versions of Heine. Except for *The North Sea*, a book written in free verse, Heine used a regular line, most often the four-beat line of German folk song, whose austerities served him as a way of purifying some of the emotional excesses of romantic poetry.

The result is that most of his verse simply chimes too much for our taste. For us, relentlessly regular verse has too long a history of humor, of irony at best and farce at worst. Palgrave's anthology, and Robert Service and company, have enervated that music. We still love and value regular verse, to be sure; but as the conflicts and the vexations of the poets more closely approach our own, we want a verse that strains against the measured line, or overflows into free verse. We prefer Keats to Byron, Wordsworth to Pope, Dickinson to Poe.

Heine himself recognized the problem. He detested the imperious strictures of French classical verse and called it "rhymed belching." The translations of his work into French that he found most satisfying were by his friend Gérard de Nerval; Nerval's versions, he said, "grasped the essence" of his poems. Nerval was a metrical poet of genius, but he translated Heine's poems into prose, into a marvelously supple, luminous prose. These are the most satisfying translations of Heine I know, but they work resolutely against the musical identity of the originals.

But there are other difficulties in trying to make Heine live for us. In his poetry and his prose, Heine depended a great deal on irony and satire, and he was often very funny. ("The despairing republican who plunges a dagger into his heart, like Brutus, may have smelt the dagger beforehand in case it had been used to cut up a herring.") We prefer our exemplary figures more somber, more solemn, even grim, even suicidal. It's hard for us to believe that a wag such as Byron could have been considered one of the most important figures of his time. And the same is true of Heine.

Despite their humor, of course, both Byron and Heine were completely, deadly serious; and in some ways Heine may have been too serious for his own good. He was generally considered as far and away the best German poet of his generation. He was enormously popular in his time and after: there are some eight thousand musical settings of his poems by twenty-five hundred composers, including Schubert, Schumann, Mendelssohn, Liszt, and Ives. He was much beloved in the German-speaking states, at least until he began to alienate his audience with his attacks on the nationalism that had made its ugly, violent, and anti-Semitic appearance both on the Right and the Left, and with the skeptical tensions of his later poetry, which made it less accessible to a public that had come to expect a romanticism whose emotional excesses he had consciously set out to purify.

He was also detested on other grounds. Carlyle called him a "slimy and greasy Jew—fit only to eat sausages made of toads." Heine was routinely vilified as a Jew, a fate that was painfully ironic to him. He never hid the fact that he was born a Jew; he was unashamedly attached to Jewish history and tradition, and he wrote a number of poems and an unfinished novel, *The Rabbi of Bacherach,* that incorporated and sometimes celebrated that history and that tradition. For most of his life, however, he was a passionate Deist, and he tended to make little of his Jewishness, as well as of his youthful conversion to Christianity. That conversion was clearly a matter of convenience, meant to qualify him for a university appointment (in law) that he never received anyway. He scorned Felix Mendelssohn for his more sincere Christian convictions: "if I had the luck of being a grandson of Moses Mendelssohn," he wrote, "I would surely not use my talent to set the pissing of the Lamb to music." But Germany was no longer the haven of tolerance that the elder Mendelssohn and his friend Lessing had thought it to be; Heine did suffer anti-Semitic attacks, and even his regular contributions to the *Augsburger Allgemeine Zeitung* were identified in the paper's editorial offices by a Star of David.

The problem present-day readers have with Heine is that, except in the disciplines of his poetic composition, he wasn't careful. He was an energetic, sometimes fanatical self-promoter, but he wasn't cunning or cold-blooded enough to care very much about the glances of posterity. His passionate earnestness about so many different issues, which made his writing so fascinating to his contemporaries, works against him as a culture hero. He could write more or less systematically about rather abstruse matters, as in his vivacious essay "On the History of Religion and Philosophy in Germany," which helped to introduce German thought to French readers. He also wrote books and articles on current political events, morals and manners, music, theater and literature, among other things. And he was not above pure and simple gossip in his reporting on the society of the French capital to his German-speaking newspaper audiences, and could be scathing in his criticism of German life in his voluminous writing for French readers.

Heine, in other words, has none of that reticence, that holding back for the effect of mystery, which in our time implies profoundity; there's not enough shadow in his light. What an advantage Kafka's circumspection gives him over a blabbermouth like Heine, who has an opinion about everything, who attacks every one, and when he is attacked himself strikes back powerfully, often changing his mind while he's at it. Heine had the unendearing habit of projecting his own shortcomings onto others, often onto his friends, and then pillorying them for their errors.

There is not even a good likeness of Heine. The extant paintings and drawings look like portraits of different people, one a rather corpulent self-absorbed aesthete, another an emaciated forlorn lover, one more a dying Christ-like martyr. Even people who knew Heine personally seemed to have manifested a puzzling uncertainty about his physical appearance. One acquaintance gives him in one place black hair and in another brown; and most people who knew him said he was dark blond. The only likeness that looks at least like *somebody*—it shows a young man with a haircut so awful that he has to have been real—is a bronze by David d'Angers, which has the disadvantage of being in relief, and lacks the character-intensifying high-contrast to which we are accustomed in images of cultural icons.

And yet Pawel succeeds admirably in bringing Heine to life. By focusing on the terrible last years, when Heine was almost completely confined to what he called his "mattress grave" but was still writing, Pawel tempers the occasional harshness of Heine's character and presents for us a writer elevated by suffering to a more exalted, stoical, self-denying level than Heine himself would have believed possible. His book has an intricate fugal structure that intercuts Heine's life with political and social events, and in this way Pawel gives a strong sense of what a turbulent, terrifically interesting epoch Heine lived through. It was a period of revolution and reaction, of social and political upheaval and spectacular economic expansion. In his books and his journalism Heine managed to situate himself at the very center of his time.

About the more intimate aspects of Heine's life, Pawel can sometimes seem a bit too partisan. Disinterestedness and objectivity are not absolute virtues in a biographer, but Pawel is often irritatingly sniffy about almost everyone—no, everyone—with whom Heine came into contact. Heine's brother Gustav, with whom "he has nothing in common other than a mother remote in every sense of the word," is "tactless, pig-headed aggressive . . . monumentally obtuse." Heine's cousin Carl, the son of his very wealthy banker uncle with whom he struggled, often in public, his whole adult life, was "a decorticate bully with no perceptible capacity for human relations . . . a troglodyte millionaire." All of Heine's family members are finally lumped together as "the gangsters to whom Heine had the misfortune of being related." Julius Campe, Heine's long-time publisher, with whom Heine had a conflicted, oedipal, but finally mostly affectionate relationship is "Mephistopheles . . . not reluctant to squeeze out what little blood was left in [Heine's] pitiable skeleton." Karl Marx "knew very little about people, including himself."

If Pawel admits for a moment that Heine's sister Charlotte's memories of him "reflect genuine sisterly love," he quickly qualifies by announcing that "they may have been somewhat prettified for the benefit of posterity." After Heine's death, his wife, whom he had rechristened Mathilde, engages "a slimy shyster of a lawyer" to represent her in the sale of Heine's papers. And the intriguing Camille Selden, the "La Mouche" who befriended Heine at the very end, becoming his secretary and his last, necessarily Platonic love-interest, was "probably neither as young or innocent as he may have believed."

By diminishing everyone around Heine, Pawel threatens to shrink Heine's own scale. And sometimes one feels like coming to the defense of the various accused. Cousin Carl, who was certainly not in perfect sympathy with his difficult poet relation, did continue for the last years of Heine's life (and the thirty years more of his widow's survival) the allowance that his father had granted Heine. And if Campe did struggle with Heine about royalties and did commit the indefensible sin for a publisher of pledging to publish anything Heine wrote and then reneging on his promise, he was also a tireless promoter of Heine's work and took chances for Heine with the German censors that clearly went beyond mere questions of profit. And Mathilde, whom Pawel all but accuses of infidelity, and whose disappearance for a month immediately after Heine's death he finds despicable and unpardonable, was a healthy young woman who, after all, lived with Heine for eight years after he had become an invalid, and sexually dysfunctional by his own account. That she would have felt released enough by the end of Heine's endless dying to leave Paris was odd, but even if she did go away, as Marx snarled, with her "pimp," we might at least try to understand her.

Pawel even manages to attack Heine, or at least his "more problematic character traits": "the flashes of paranoia, the unrestrained viciousness of his personal attacks on enemies or friends he felt had wronged him, his propensity to desecrate his pen . . . in . . . infantile temper tantrums." In all the standard studies of Heine—the best is *Heinrich Heine, a Modern Biography* by Jeffrey L. Sammons—we get the sense that Heine was a difficult person. He was constantly provoking scandals and was thin-skinned enough to have been involved in a number of duels, but he was also endlessly interesting, "a man of unruly but noble character," as he himself said of Liszt. Though he seemed to have few intimate friends, he knew everyone, from Goethe to Balzac, from Chopin to Wagner, from George Sand to Hans Christian Andersen, from Marx to the Rothschilds. In his youth he worshiped Napoleon and adored all that the French Revolution stood for; but in the course of his life he had to witness its ideals betrayed, in the reaction of 1830 and the more serious conservative triumph after the 1848 turmoil, which he seemed almost unable to bring himself to behold, so much a violation was it of his old aspirations.

Though he consistently managed to offend popular notions of decorum, both personal and political, he was a passionate democrat, and one of the clear purposes of his poetry and prose was to undermine bourgeois and aristocratic hypocrisy, to make a literature that would be more accessible and more truthful. He wrote variations of old fairy tales, which he believed incorporated lost popular wisdom, and generated new ones. (Wagner used two of his poems, "Tannhäuser" and "The Flying Dutch-man," as the basis of operas, and later, as his anti-Semitism became virulent, repudiated his debt to Heine. The Nazis, when they burned Heine's books and banished him from the antholo-gies, had to preserve "Lorelei" under "author unknown," be-cause the poem had become so integral a part of the German national identity.)

Heine said he didn't approve of "political poetry," because he felt that nearly all the polemical poetry of his time was tainted by the rot of nationalism, but most of his work was profoundly engaged. He wrote the most effective and enduring German political poem of the century, "The Silesian Weavers," which became an anthem for disaffected workers. (Engels translated it into English.) And he even composed a poem about the slave trade to the Americas, "The Slave Ship," one of his few poems that comes into English with no excuses. (Both works are in-cluded in the Pawel volume, in a sheaf of poems appended to the text. Pawel reprints the Hal Draper versions of the poems to which he refers, a useful device in a biography of a poet.)

"The Slave Ship" is brilliant, an almost surreal narrative about a slave-trader in despair because the profits of his Rio-bound ship are threatened by his cargo dying off. The ship's doctor diagnoses the problem by saying that it's the blacks' "own fault," that their "melancholia . . . bores them to death." He prescribes music and dancing for the slaves, and in a scene like something from a wilder *Benito Cereno,* the slaves dance and make love as music is played by the crew, as sharks prowl below, wondering why they haven't received their usual breakfast of dead slaves, and the captain prays:

> Oh, spare their lives for Jesus' sake
> Who did not die in vain!
> If I don't end up with three hundred head,
> My business goes down the drain.

Though he never participated directly in any of the great politi-cal upheavals of his time, he observed them and commented on them with a fierce independence. He was a man of the Left, a liberal, and was even a Saint-Simonian for a period when he first came to visit Paris in 1831, before he was definitively exiled from the German states; and he always shared with the Left a genuine indignation at the mistreatment of the common people. In his work, however, he was mistrustful of both Right and Left, and his refusal to take definitive positions left him, as his sometime friend Ludwig Borne noted, with "two backs," abused by both aristocratic and radical factions.

The various governments of the German-speaking states felt threatened enough by his writing to ban most of his books (Metternich made it a personal cause) and finally to banish Heine himself from their borders; and so he lived the last twenty-five years of his life in France. But most of the radicals considered him inadequately revolutionary, and he was as trenchant about the Left as about the Right, and as prescient. "Communism," he wrote, "is the secret name, the frightful antagonist which opposes to the contemporary bourgeois regime proletarian rule with all its consequences . . . The dismal hero to whom is assigned a great, if only temporary role in the modern tragedy." He was drawn to rabble-rousers like Cobbett; but when Cobbett printed a scurrilous anti-Semitic attack, Heine was confirmed in his fears that popular radicalism would generate such monstrosities.

But the project of his writing really went beyond all that. Heine's aesthetic and spiritual purpose was what he called "sensualism," a reassertion of the rights of matter and the body, in art and society. He called for a poetry of "the most self-intoxicated subjectivity, world-unbridled individuality, the divinely free personality with all its love of life." He was like Whitman in his vision of a society in which art and poetry would free the individual from ancient habits of social passivity, and increase the dimensions and intensity of human aspiration and emotion. (Whitman exulted, "Heine was free . . . one of the men who win by degrees.") If Heine's poems and songs were often about lost love, that love was never the bloodless aristocratic nostalgia of romanticism: it was rich with physicality and erotic ardor. There are scores of love affairs in his poems, and scores of women. He sings of escapades with the most timid maidens and the boldest matrons: one poem recounts a memorable adventure with a mother and a daughter.

Given the larger ends that he saw for his poetry, it is ironic (and he thought so, too) that the greater part of his fame rested on those gorgeous songs that concerned a few probably fictional amorous episodes of his youth. He considered the poetic perfection of those songs an essential part of his moral undertaking, but he sometimes sounds almost plaintive in trying to reassert the depths of his commitment to his social ideals. "Whether people praise or fault my songs concerns me little. But you shall lay a sword on my coffin, for I was a good soldier in mankind's war of liberation."

That coffin was hard-earned. Heine died a truly terrifying death—from syphilis, he thought, though modern medicine has cast doubt upon that diagnosis. Parts of his body were paralyzed, restored to use and paralyzed again, and finally he became a helpless invalid, a living skeleton, racked with pain through most of his last eight years, finding relief only in morphine, which was administered to him through sores kept open for that purpose on his back. To read or write, he often had to hold one of his eyelids propped open, and sometimes he could hardly speak. But despite all this, and despite the stream of visitors that came from all over Europe to pay homage to the world-famous poet, he wrote, and wrote, and wrote: poetry during his mostly sleepless nights, prose the rest of the time.

The report of Heine's final moments should certainly be inscribed in the book of last words said *to* the dying. Trying to the very end to write, he kept asking his nurse to take dictation. She couldn't, but reassured him: "When you stop throwing up, you'll write yourself." It is a shock to realize that when he did finally die, he was fifty-eight. Pawel accomplishes the deathbed transformation that Heine himself mocked and despised: by the end he seems reinvested with a kind of innocence; his fantasy love-affair with "La Mouche" has about it the pathetic mortal longing of Keats for his Fanny. The ordeal of his dying burned off much of Heine's desperate narcissism and at least some of the sardonic cruelty that could afflict his skepticism.

But that skepticism was always less savage than it appeared. In a poem occasioned by a visit to Heine's grave, Matthew Arnold caustically wrote that Heine had been destined "only to laugh and to die." This is unfair. Heine's edge was the edge of a great humanist. Indeed, there was so much hope for humanity in

Heine's criticism that it seems almost religious in its impulse. The converted Jew who was a dedicated Deist for most of his life returned finally to a personal God, in whom he claimed to believe with a childlike simplicity but toward whom he was not entirely affectionate: "... this great tormentor of animals," he called him. But Heine's mature spiritual convictions were clearly grounded in his skepticism. The fury of his attacks on human folly and human cruelty were animated by a profound affirmation, a cry against the disappointments that so much of the history he lived had brought him.

Our own skepticism is even more fretful and thoroughgoing than his. History has proved even darker than Heine believed it to be, and the affirmations we salvage from it have been tempered by grimmer denials than he could have imagined, despite his famous prophecy that where books are burned, people will be burned, too. When we contemplate the energy with which Heine lived and the admirable stoicism of his dying, when we study his poetry, which even in translation begins to regenerate the music of its fervent intentions, he does indeed become heroic, a writer of enormous moral and intellectual power, an ardent and inspiring idealist.

Miklós Radnóti

I fell beside him. His body rolled over,
as tight as a string ready to snap.
Shot in the neck. "You'll end the same way,"
I whispered to myself. "Lie still."
Now patience flowers into death.
"Der springt noch auf," I heard someone say.
Blood dried on my ear, and filthy clay.

On October 8, 1944, the Hungarian poet Miklós Radnóti watched as his friend and fellow labor camp prisoner, the violinist Miklós Lorsi, was shot by the S.S., then shot again—"Der springt noch auf" ("He's still kicking")—finally to death, as three thousand inmates were being marched toward Germany, ahead of the advancing Allied armies, from the labor camp Lager Heidenau in Yugoslavia. This poem, the last of a series by Radnóti called "Postcards," which were all composed along that terrible trek, was dated October 31. The next to the last was from October 24:

Bloody drool hangs on the mouths of the oxen.
The men all piss red.
The company stands around in stinking wild knots.
Death blows overhead, disgusting.
                    (Translated by Polgar, Berg, and Marks)

The six thousand prisoners in Lager Heidenau had been divided into two groups, and Radnóti had gone to great lengths to be part of the first. Perhaps he thought that he would have more of a chance to survive that way. Or perhaps, as some of his friends surmised, he was simply impatient to return to his wife, his high school sweetheart, on whom he doted and for whom he wrote some of his most moving poems:

> I've been planning to tell you
> about the secret galaxy of my love for so long—
> in just one image, just the essence.
> But you are swarming and flooding inside me like
> existence, as eternal and certain sometimes
> as a snail shell changed to stone inside a stone.
>
> (Translated by Polgar et al.)

"I fell beside him. His body rolled over." There is an ambiguity in that last "Postcard" poem. Is someone else dying, or is it, as it seems on first reading, that Radnóti is beholding and enacting and making poetry of his own death? I think both. His death, which came on November 8 or 9, was to be frighteningly similar, and even more poignantly absurd. Radnóti was part of a group of twenty-one exhausted prisoners who were put under the guard neither of the S.S., nor of their ferociously anti-Semitic Hungarian counterparts, the Arrow-Cross, but of a squad of Hungarian sergeants. The apparently uninterested soldiers twice tried to turn their wards over to crowded local hospitals but were turned away. Finally they simply shot the prisoners and buried them in a common grave. Of the three thousand prisoners in Radnóti's group who began the march toward Germany, only a fraction survived. The other three thousand were soon liberated by Tito's partisans. Radnóti's body was exhumed eighteen months later. The five last poems, and five others as brilliant and as moving, which had been composed in the Lager and had already been delivered to his widow by a friend, were found in a notebook in his overcoat pocket.

Those poems, and the others Radnóti composed toward the end of his life, and the story of his outrageous death, have all become a part of the literature of evidence of the Holocaust. Our need for that evidence seems limitless. We read one poem or one book on the Holocaust, we read hundreds, and each, in its engrossing unlikeliness, in its terrible undeniability, seems as essential as the first. In some ways the Holocaust has become for us almost a convention. The cruelty, the murder, the blood, the fear, are like notes on a scale; what we hear are threnodies in an established mode.

At the same time, there is something about these liturgies of shame that isn't susceptible in any ordinary way to the imagination, in the sense that imagination is the fusion of the moral and the mental, of the mind as agent and the matter of the mind as subject; they simply won't allow the resolution, the solidity, the sense of being set, that is generally achieved by phenomena imagination has confronted. We seem to have to begin our moral education again each time we encounter that history. This is reality, the gas chamber; this is truth, the perfectly arbitrary bullet. And so we read again, as though we would, if we could accumulate enough of the gruesome particulars, finally "understand," finally be allowed the kind of closure and consummation our other histories bring us.

And yet, when we are dealing with the evidence left by an artist, there can be something unjust in all this. To define a dedicated poet like Radnóti merely, or primarily, or even partially as a witness is to violate the meaning that he gave his own life, and his own death. Radnóti was a poet. If, under the pressure of events, his pure and passionate poetry was forced to incorporate the horrors with which his world was afflicted, it did so resolutely in the context of his commitment to the lyric.

He was born in 1909. Hungary, "that little country ringed by fire," as he would call it in a late poem, was already, by the time he reached maturity, in a state of incipient explosion. Radnóti's life wasn't particularly unusual for that time. Born into a nonobservant Jewish family, his early years were marked by tragedy that was personal rather than public: the death of his mother and a twin brother at his birth, and of his father when he was twelve. In *Under Gemini*, an autobiographical memoir, he recounts the shattering experience of discovering that his mother was his stepmother and his sister his half sister. (In all of Radnóti's books in English, it is remarked only in one edition, in a footnote to a poem from the 1940s, that the stepmother and half sister both died at Auschwitz. Radnóti never knew it.)

Hungary in the 1920s and 1930s, traumatized by the disastrous peace treaty after World War I and an unfortunate period under a "Soviet" government, was undergoing, like much of Europe, a period of intense anti-Semitism. The country was, if anything, ahead of Germany, at least early on, in promulgating racial laws, with the result that Radnóti was forced to attend university in Szeged rather than in Budapest, where the Jewish quota had already been filled. He studied Hungarian and French literature, became active in leftist university politics, and had already published three books of poetry by the time he received his doctorate in 1935. By then any religious interest he may have had seemed to have been directed toward the Catholicism that attracted so many intellectuals during the 1930s, but his Jewish origins proscribed him from the teaching positions for which he was qualified. He tutored instead, taught in his father-in-law's stenography school, translated, and generally lived the pinched but not yet desperate existence of a writer in the thriving cultural life of Budapest *entre deux guerres.*

He was in Paris in 1931, then again in 1937, when he was a spectator at a literary congress in which the participants included Neruda, Brecht, and Langston Hughes. Paris remained a powerful lure for him; he used it often in his poems as a symbol of "elsewhere." He was there again in 1939 and must have considered staying or fleeing further. He had already written, though, of the risks of exile. "In a cheap New York hotel / T tied a rope around his neck. He walked around homeless for many years. How can he go on?" "T" was Ernst Toller, the German playwright.

Hungary threw in its lot with Germany in 1939, and Radnóti's situation became much darker. Before his fatal exile in 1944, he was sent away in 1941 to clear mines and barbed wire from areas that Hungary had reacquired from Romania, then again in 1943 for a period of brutal labor in a sugar beet refinery. His poems were no longer published after 1938, although he continued to translate, and to compose at an ever more intense pace.

Radnóti's early poems were heavily influenced by various avant-garde movements, particularly the French. His political leftism also left its mark: many of the poems from his first books enact a self-conscious, almost programmatically "proletarian" sensual openness. But there is always something good-tempered and large-spirited in the work. It almost echoes Whitman in its insistence on an open sexuality, in its attempt to fuse the spiritual and the frankly erotic. This was not the sort of thing to please an authoritarian, puritanical regime, always on the look-out for a Jew to scapegoat. Radnóti's second book was confiscated, and in 1931 he went on trial for "effrontery to public modesty and incitement to rebellion."

Although he received a sentence of only a few days, this was a matter of moment, because it further threatened Radnóti's already precarious professional prospects, and he fought to have the verdict reversed—successfully, as it turned out, mostly because of the influence of a Catholic priest who had been his mentor at Szeged. Radnóti afterward toned down the direct sensuality in his poems, but he was the kind of poet anyway whose successes have less to do with the material of the poems than with their poetic and lyric intensity. From his earliest work, Radnóti was primarily a pastoralist, a love poet, a singer. Even during the earliest experimental period, the poems usually work through the protocols of nature consciousness, of an ecstatic voice moving through orthodox landscape, in conventional protestations of passion. Although his work was informed from start to finish with a deep moral generosity, when he allowed his political concerns to come openly into his work, as in the poems he wrote about the Spanish War, they usually sit awkwardly:

> Freedom men cry about your fate!
> This afternoon, they sang for you.
> With heavy words, the wet-faced poor
> of Paris sang about your battles.
>
> (Translated by Polgar et al.)

This isn't at all to say that Radnóti was ever less than a single-minded, self-conscious artist. He studied assiduously in the literatures of the several languages he knew, and translated extensively, from French (Ronsard, La Fontaine, Apollinaire, Cendars, Larbaud) and German (some of the classical poets, Rilke, Trakl) and English (Blake, Wordsworth, and *Twelfth Night*). He was working on his translation of Shakespeare when he was sent away for the last time. He read Whitman; he knew, intensely admired, and wrote several times about Lorca, whose work he read in English. More openly in the early work, but later on as well, there are traces of many of these poets. Even the harrowing "Postcards" have their genesis in experiments by Apollinaire and Cendars.

Radnóti's most admired translation is the "Ninth Eclogue" of Virgil, which was also important in the development of his own work. After it he began his own series of eclogues, and they are among the most masterful of his poems. Working in a form so closely associated with the pastoral seems paradoxically to have released him into more encompassing poetic reflections. "The First Eclogue," a dialogue between a poet and a shepherd, written in 1938, is also the first of his poems in which the horror of contemporary events comes into the poem without feeling forced or intrusive. The Shepherd says:

> What I heard is now certain: amid corpses stiff with blood,
> On the ridges of the wild Pyrenees, red-hot cannon wrangle . . .
> In flocks, with knotted bundles, flee old folk, women and
> children,
> Throwing themselves on the ground as
> Death starts circling above,
> And there are so many lying dead.
>
> (Translated by Wilmer and Gömöri)

"The Second Eclogue" is a dialogue between a poet and a pilot, both of whom are stoically aware that they will probably soon die. "Will you write about me?" the pilot asks. "If I'm alive," the poet responds, "If there's anyone left." It is hardly surprising that the premonition of violent death should be such a prominent theme in the poems of this period. "I am the only they'll kill finally, / because I myself never killed," one says. But right to the end there is still always something wonderfully pure about Radnóti's work. The character of the poet in the work is frank, open, essentially healthy. Even in the poem called "Maybe," in which the possibility of going mad is meditated, there is a "palinode":

> Don't leave me, delicate mind!
>   Don't let me go crazy.
> Sweet wounded reason, don't
>   leave me now.
> (Translated by Polgar et al.)

And in a poem even more grim, "The Terrifying Angel" (which echoes Rilke's *Duino Elegies*), a poem on suicide, in which the madness, driven by a reality itself demented, seems much closer, the power of the poetry still sublimates the sentiments of death, so that the speculation, though driven and desperate, still has nothing of the neurotic about it:

> Here, here's the knife.
> It doesn't hurt. It takes only a second, there's only a hiss . . .
> And the knife woke up on the table and flashed.
> (Translated by Polgar et al.)

It is its lyric power that makes much of the later work's intense confrontation with the dismal actualities Radnóti was living so effective. The poems become more and more formally intricate, rhymed and metered; this, combined with the way he charged them with both general and personal anguish, gives them the feeling of being almost driven out of their own definitions. The pastoral is forced to the very limits of the serenity to which it still stubbornly bears evidence. A love poem can become a study of violated consciousness, of the mind hounded to the state at which it is tempted to try to escape itself. In another poem addressed to his wife, he writes:

> Do you see night, the wild oakwood fence lined with barbed
>   wire,
> and the barracks, so flimsy that the night swallowed them?
> Slowly the eye passes the limits of captivity
> and only the mind, the mind knows how
> tight the wire is.
> You see, dear, this is how we set our imaginations free.
>   (Translated by Polgar et al.)

Toward the end, the poems become ever more conflicted and anguished. The anger Radnóti was so conscious of keeping out of his work—"There's no anger in my heart right now, I don't think about revenge"—emerges despite him, and a prophetic note begins to inform the work:

> I lived on this earth in an age
> when man fell so low
> he killed willingly, for pleasure, without orders . . .
> . . . Drunk on blood and scum, the nation went mad
> and grinned at its horrible fate.
>   (Translated by Polgar et al.)

Or:

> There are boys crouching. Awkward pretty words
> stick to their lips like embers.
> Their bodies swell with many little victories.
> Calmly, when they have to,
> they kill.
>   (Translated by Polgar et al.)

Radnóti composed poems, astonishingly, all during his last term in the camp, sometimes in despair, sometimes in resignation. In a poem called "Root," he says,

> I am a root myself now,
> living among worms.
> This poem is written down there.
>
> > (Translated by Polgar et al.)

And in "A Letter to My Wife," he cries out, "I know you are my friend, my wife . . . you are three wild borders away!" If Radnóti was ever tempted by the consolations of religion, it shows hardly at all in his poetry, and yet he turns, in the last and eighth eclogue, to the Old Testament as a source for what has now become spiritual fury. In a dialogue with the prophet Nahum, the poet says:

> Whole nations scramble to the slaughter,
> And the soul of Man is stripped bare, even as Nineveh . . .
> . . . Of all beasts, Man is the basest!
> Here, tiny babes are dashed against walls and, over there,
> The church tower is a torch, the house an oven roasting
> Its own people.
>
> > (Translated by Wilmer and Gömöri)

He is being worn down, the poet says, "like a round stone in a wild stream," and the prophet, in a kind of pardon, or a kind of condolence, answers:

> So you may think. But I know your new poems. Wrath nurtures
>   you.
> The poet's wrath, much like the prophet's, is food and drink
> To the people.
>
> > (Translated by Wilmer and Gömöri)

Even after that, though, with only weeks to live, it is the lyric to which Radnóti returns. The first two of the terrible "Postcards" reaffirm the humility, the power, and the unlikely formal calm of Radnóti's lyricism. This is the first:

> From Bulgaria the huge wild pulse of artillery.
> It beats on the mountain ridge, then hesitates, falls.

Men, animals, wagons, and thoughts. They are swelling.
The road whinnies and rears. The sky gallops.
You are permanent within me in this chaos.
Somewhere deep in my mind you shine forever, without
moving, silent, like the angel awed by death,
or like the insect burying itself
in the rotted heart of a tree.

And the second:

Nine miles from here
the haystacks and houses burn,
and on the edges of the meadow
there are quiet frightened peasants, smoking.
The little shepherd girl seems
to step into the lake, the water ripples.
The ruffled sheepfold
bends to the clouds and drinks.

(Both translated by Polgar et al.)

What exactly is the poet doing when he inscribes those last postcards from the provinces of death, when he wills himself to impose form on reality as close to chaos as anything ever inflicted on our sad planet? Common knowledge would say that art serves something beyond itself, that it is an implement, of morality, of belief. But for the artist it is actually everything else that serves art. This is the wisdom of art, the knowledge that beauty perhaps is the one undeniably unique attribute of the human. That a man, already condemned to an abyss of ferocious irrationality, should will his soul toward the seemingly gratuitous beauties of precision and form is metaphysically ludicrous, but exalting.

When we read Radnóti's poems, we sense all this, the struggle with form, the dedication and the affirmation, and we are reflected back to ourselves out of the graceful and still serene whisperings between consciousness and its medium. The blood is drying on that dying, or already dead, ear; but the ear still hears the music it is making for itself and for us. Radnóti is a great poet, and his work brings us moving witness of courage, tenacity, and spiritual defiance. But the real triumph of his poetry is the way that it constrains the appalling evidence to work for its own purposes, the way that it testifies to the redemptive resources of the poetic imagination. Its triumph, finally, is itself.

Some Notes on Hopkins

1

I thought at first only a trick of memory made me believe that one of the first poems I ever really attached to while I was in college was Gerard Manley Hopkins's "Windhover." How unreasonable it seems now that as inexperienced a reader as I was in those days could understand, no less be mysteriously moved by, such an apparently forbidding series of phrases:

> I caught this morning morning's minion, king-
>> dom of daylight's dauphin, dapple-dáwn-drawn Falcon, in his
>>> riding
>> Of the rólling level úndernéath him steady áir, and stríding
> High there, how he rung upon the rein of a wimpling wing
> In his ecstasy! then off, off forth on swing,
>> As a skate's heel sweeps smooth on a bow-bend, the hurl and
>>> gliding
>> Rebuffed the big wind. My heart in hiding
> Stirred for a bird,—the achieve of, the mastery of the thing!

Such strange linkages, such self-consciously elusive diction; such unfamiliar music: the concussive, unpredictable stresses, the movement of the voice almost breathless, itself rolling and striding. And the meaning! All those turbulent metaphors, melting into one another, transfiguring, complicating each other. The sense seems almost impossible to follow, it is as though the diction were trying to distract the concentration rather than focus it. Did I really understand what the poem meant? Do I yet?

I did, I knew I did, and I still do, although if I had to make too systematic an explication of the poem, I'd probably be bored. As I would if I had to analyze with too much intellectual attention "Henry Purcell," with its plaintive, insistent sublimations of aesthetic regret, its barely contained swells of artistic identification and admiration:

> Have fáir fállen, O fáir O fáir have fállen, so déar
> To me, so arch-especial a spirit as heaves in Henry Purcell,
> An age is now since passed, since parted; with the reversal
> Of the outward sentence low lays him, listed to a heresy, here.

I was sure even then that I didn't understand these poems as I'd been taught I was supposed to, but that may have partly been what drew me to them. Something was happening to me as I read that had nothing to do with "understanding," but whatever was happening, I wanted more of it, and there was a lot more, just as strange, just as intense, just as much apparently out at the edges of rational discourse, and just as thrilling:

> The world is charged with the grandeur of God.
> It will flame out, like shining from shook foil;
>   It gathers to a greatness like the ooze of oil
> Crushed.
>
> ("God's Grandeur")

> Felix Randal the farrier, O is he déad then? my dúty all énded,
> Who have watched his mould of man, big-boned and hardy-
>   handsome
> Pining, pining, till time when reason rambled in it and some
> Fatal four disorders, fleshed there, all contended?
>
> ("Felix Randal")

At first glance, I knew, though I didn't know how I knew, exactly how to work my way through the delicate metaphysical figuration of "The Wreck of the Deutschland":

> I am sóft sift
> In an hourglass—at the wall
> Fast, but mined with a motion, a drift,
> And it crowds and it combs to the fall;
> I steady as a water in a well, to a poise, to a pane,

> But roped with, always, all the way down from the tall
> Fells or flanks of the voel, a vein
> Of the gospel proffer, a pressure, a principle, Christ's gift.

I even could grasp, however inchoately, the passionate metaphysical doubt of "Carrion Comfort":

> Not, I'll not, carrion comfort, Despair, not feast on thee;
> Not untwist—slack they may be—these last strands of man
> In me ór, most weary, cry I can no more. I can;
> Can something, hope, wish day come, not choose not to be.

It seems entirely unlikely, but Hopkins, a Jesuit priest, a solitary, tormented soul, and one of the most radical innovators in the history of English poetry, left a body of work that is among the most seductive in the language, one many readers find themselves taken with before they really quite understand why. Perhaps it's not so surprising, though: there's something immediately welcoming about the poems, despite their surface complexity; they catch the ear, come readily into consciousness, ring compelling and true, and are surprisingly easy to commit to memory.

They hold, too. Whenever I come back to Hopkins, I'm surprised at how integral a part of my poetic cosmology his work is. In the most basic way, the poems, for all their audacity, for all their density and strangeness, remain exciting, and *trustworthy,* somehow; they are, to use one of Hopkin's own favorite terms, lovable.

2

Hopkins was born in 1844 into what still is the very model of a large and lucky family: a father who was a solidly well-off but not disturbingly wealthy marine insurance adjustor, a sensitive and attentive mother, eight siblings, and comfortable houses with servants. The family was artistically inclined, much given to amateur theatrics, charades, and entertainments. Hopkins's father was something of a minor Renaissance man: he sketched, composed songs, and wrote: a history of Hawaii (he acted for a number of years as consul general for Hawaii in London); an unpublished novel; essays and literary criticism for various periodicals; and three published if decidedly second-rate, volumes of poetry. One of Hopkins's aunts was an artist, and an uncle initiated him into the esoterics of the new art of photography. Two of Hopkins's brothers became illustrators, and one sister was a gifted amateur musician. Hopkins himself sketched and late in his life began to compose music.

But still, in all that Victorian glow of domestic creativity, there must have been some darker tensions. None of Hopkins's sisters ever married, and among all the children, Hopkins felt close to only one of his brothers. And there was the matter of Hopkins's conversion.

While a student at Oxford, Hopkins announced to his startled, piously Anglican parents that he was converting to Roman Catholicism and, shortly after, distressed them further by informing them of his intention to become a Jesuit priest.

It's hard now to realize how much open animus there still was in Protestant Europe during the nineteenth century toward Roman Catholicism and toward the Jesuits in particular. When Hopkins was finishing university, before he entered the order, he took the opportunity to travel in Switzerland; he would no longer be able to afterward because Jesuits weren't allowed past the country's frontiers. In the years he was at Oxford, Roman Catholics were still banned from taking an MA and had only recently been allowed to practice their religion in the context of the university community.

At the time Hopkins matriculated, Oxford had been the center of a serious, decades-long debate between liberal and conservative religious thinkers. The period was similar in some ways to the 1930s in America, when the seductions of radical thought generated a religious counterreaction among intellectuals and students, with a similar wave of Roman Catholic conversions.

Hopkins, who had been since childhood a devout Anglican, moved during his university years toward a more and more conservative position, arriving finally at a belief in what he called the "real presence" of divinity in the Roman Catholic ritual. "I can hardly believe anyone ever became a Catholic because two and two make four more fully than I have," he wrote at the time of his conversion, and later, in a letter to his friend and fellow poet Robert Bridges, he expressed the depth of his convictions: "You do not mean by mystery what a Catholic does, you mean an interesting uncertainty: the uncertainty ceasing interest ceases also. . . . A Catholic by mystery means an incomprehensible certainty."

For all his passion, though, there was in Hopkins's conversion at least a hint of adolescent rebellion. He hadn't even informed his parents that he was considering becoming a Roman Catholic, and when he finally did notify them of his decision, he responded to their shock with a certain degree of self-righteous irritability. To his parents, his conversion and his intention to become a Jesuit must have been the equivalent of a hasty and ill-advised marriage—Hopkins was giving up any hope of the brilliant academic career for which he had seemed so well suited—but Hopkins abruptly responded to their chagrin by announcing that the Roman Catholic church "strictly forbids all communion in sacred things with non-Catholics." Although Hopkins and his parents reconciled, there seems to have been an edge of something unresolved in his relations with them, particularly with his father.

Hopkins rarely spoke of his father's slight accomplishments at verse, but it certainly would have had a complicated meaning for him. He did, in fact, copy out some of his father's work, and at least one of his early poems shows his father's influence. Hopkins himself began writing poetry very early and won a prize at his school with the precocious "The Escorial." Although when he became a Jesuit, he destroyed most of his recent poetry— "the slaughter of the innocents," he called it—and didn't write verse for the first seven years of his career as a clergyman, he came back to composition eagerly when a superior suggested he attempt a poem on the death in a shipwreck of a group of German nuns, in which Hopkins had taken a great interest. "The Wreck of the Deutschland," his most ambitious poem, was the result, and if Hopkins had not actually been composing verse for those seven years, he had undoubtedly been reflecting upon it: the poem embodies his mature style fully realized, and one might wonder whether the "slaughter" of his earlier poems had come as much from dissatisfaction as from a sense that the vocations of poet and priest were incompatible.

Even when he had dedicated himself to poetry again, Hopkins occasionally felt a conflict between his two callings. Near the end of his life, he wrote in a retreat note: "Today I earnestly asked our Lord to watch over my compositions, not to preserve them from being lost or coming to nothing, for that I am very willing they should, but they might not do me harm through the enmity or imprudence of any man or my own; that he would have them as his own and employ or not employ them as he would see fit." His relation to a potential audience for his work was ambivalent as well. He was disappointed when "The Wreck of the Deutschland" was rejected by a Jesuit magazine, but except for a few halfhearted and unsuccessful attempts to publish other poems, he was content to leave his chances of literary immortality in the hands of Bridges and a few other friends. That he didn't, however, think of himself as completely isolated from a hypothetical public is clear from the professionalism of many of his comments on his poems. He once fancied how "Harry Ploughman" would sound "recited by a chorus" and to Bridges once wrote, "I would have you . . . and all true poets remember that fame, the being known, though in itself one of the most dangerous things to man, is nevertheless the true and appointed air, element, and setting of genius and its works." Bridges, though skeptical of Hopkins's poetics, dutifully collected his work, often copying out poems of which there existed only the manuscript Hopkins sent him. Hopkins appreciated Bridges's efforts but gave the impression of being serenely indifferent to the fate of his work.

His intimate, emotional life, on the other hand, was anything but serene; it was charged with almost constant conflict. Hopkins had always been frail, high-strung, and hard on himself. He suffered a great deal from what we would call repressed sexual feelings and castigated himself for the attraction he felt toward male beauty. His career as a priest was never very successful, and he never found a situation that quite fitted his sensitivities and talents. In Liverpool and Glasgow, where he was assigned as a parish priest, he was appalled by the poverty and dissipation of his parishioners. Later, in his anguish over the brutal social divisions of industrial England, he would go so far as to suggest that he might at heart be a "communist." He well knew he wasn't, but the term captured his indignation, and many of his poems exhibit a similar sympathy toward the poor and oppressed: "Tom Garland" is subtitled "Upon the Unemployed."

Hopkins's sympathies, though, didn't seem to have helped

him in his dealings with his parishioners. His sermons were either incomprehensible to them or embarrassingly intimate. He fared little better among his intellectual peers. Although Hopkins had been a notably brilliant scholar at Oxford, when he returned to a Jesuit seminary to prepare for a career teaching young priests, a position that would certainly have suited him, he did insufficiently well on an examination to continue his studies.

Hopkins never complained about the way he was treated by the Jesuit hierarchy, manifesting instead the admirable if sometimes exasperating obedience that was a particular point of pride among the Jesuits, but it was clear he was rarely content. He suffered from depressions and from various physical ailments that were probably psychogenic. He endured a hemorrhoid operation, then a circumcision, and often complained of digestive difficulties and extreme fatigue. The Jesuits demanded much of their young men; the life expectancy of a Jesuit priest at the time was only forty-four years, as compared to sixty-one for other men. In Dublin, where Hopkins passed the last years of his life teaching classics at University College, he was often in real despair. His teaching load was enormous—he had to mark between thirteen and eighteen hundred examination papers a year—and his relationship with his usually uninterested and unruly students was for the most part unrewarding.

During the bleak years in Ireland, Hopkins often spoke of the "waste" his time there had been, and he hinted at a similar bleak feeling about his life as a whole. Although he never seemed to have faltered in his religious convictions—even the poem he wrote near the end, the so-called "terrible sonnets,"[1] never call into question his relationship with God, only with the quality of his belief, and with the need for a release from his inner torment—he was in a state of more or less constant dejection. Ortega y Gasset once opined about Goethe that he might have inflicted the wrong life on the character, the "I," he actually inhabited, and the same thing might well be said about Hopkins.

---

1. The "terrible sonnets," or "sonnets of desolation," are the series that includes "Carrion Comfort," and those which begin, "To seem the stranger," "I wake and feel," "No worst," "Patience, hard thing," and "My own heart."

There is something tragic in his convoluted and introspective genius, especially if he is compared to a writer of similar intellectual and artistic talents like Thomas Merton, whose religious conversion came at about the same age as Hopkins's and in a similar historical moment, but who found tranquility and creative release as a monastic contemplative.

But perhaps these considerations are always unfair. There was something finally heroic, almost Kierkegaardian in Hopkins's struggle with himself, with the forms of spirit that had been offered to him. Moreover, his poems often reveal a rapture, a sheer innocent delight in existence that belies his depressions, even his fearsome description of himself as "time's eunuch." The last of the terrible sonnets, written shortly before he died of typhoid in Dublin in 1889, hints at a new gentleness in his dealings with himself. It is a plea to his God, but a rare plea, too, for himself:

> My own heart let me more have pity on; let
> Me live to my sad self hereafter kind,
> Charitable; not live this tormented mind
> With this tormented mind tormenting yet.

3

Hopkins wrote often about his poetry, in letters to his friends and once in a preface to a projected but unrealized volume of his poems. Almost everything he ever said about it, though, had to do with his metrical experiments in what he called "sprung rhythm," which became a sort of screen for his even more radical approaches to the poetic imagination, to perception, cognition, and consciousness. When Hopkins discussed his work, he sounded like nothing more than the scholar and classics professor that he was, and only in his journals and retreat notes does he manifest the kind of passion and conflicted emotions that inform his poetry.

In the attempt to "convert," as he put it, the never quite wholly convinced (and Anglican) Bridges to the methods of his poems, Hopkins expounded at great length on his metrical ideas, trying to demonstrate their theoretical soundness. Probably because of this, and because he did speak so little of more substantive matters concerning his work, there has been an enormous amount of often confusing critical attention paid to Hopkins's metrical theories.

In truth, though, Hopkins's basic metrical ideas are not unreasonably intricate or arcane. In one succinct description of sprung rhythm, he wrote, "It consists in scanning by accents or stresses alone, without any account of the number of syllables, so that a foot may be one strong syllable or it may be many light and one strong."

Although as time went on, his ideas about the recitation of his verse became more and more complex—he went so far as to develop an elaborate system of performance notation—Hopkins was most likely working, as do most poets, as much from an intuitive sense of the possibilities of verse as from any preconceived theoretical position. "I had long had haunting my ear the echo of a new rhythm," he said once, and was probably most frank when he commented, "Sprung rhythm makes verse very *stressy*" (my italics). That stressiness is really what is most striking in his metrics. Although the poems' music is marked by an exuberant, almost obsessive, use of rhyme, assonance, vowel play, and alliteration, what finally makes them rhythmically unique is the abundance of stressed syllables, the verse's intensely spondaic sense of itself. Stress, Hopkins once said, "purges [poetry] to an emphasis as much brighter, livelier, more lustrous than the regular but commonplace emphasis of common rhythm as poetry in general is brighter than common speech." And that stressy luster is certainly evident in, for instance, the beginning of "Spelt from Sibyl's Leaves":

> Earnest, earthless, equal, attuneable, | vaulty, voluminous, . . .
>   stupendous
> Evening strains to be tímes vást, | womb-of-all, home-of-all,
>   hearse-of-all night.

While Hopkins was conscious of the singular effects of his poetry—"no doubt my poetry errs on the side of oddness," he would say—he claimed to have had no wish to violate the norms of common speech. In a statement surprisingly like Wordsworth's a few generations before, Hopkins tells Bridges that he uses sprung rhythm "because it is the nearest to the rhythm of prose, that is the native and natural of speech, the least forced, the most rhetorical and emphatic of all possible rhythms, combining as it seems to me, opposite and one would have thought incompatible excellences, markedness of rhythm . . . and naturalness of expression."

Like many innovators, Hopkins was ambivalent about his originality. He could be fiercely jealous of it—"The effect of studying masterpieces," he once said, "is to make me admire and do otherwise"—but could also be more realistic: "I do not say the idea [of sprung rhythm] is altogether new; there are hints of it in music, in nursery rhymes and popular jingles, and in the poets themselves. . . . But no one has professedly used it and made it the principle throughout, that I know of." (In fact, Coleridge had elaborated a remarkably similar principle for "Christabel," although with quite different results.)

As is the case with most poets, Hopkins's relation to his peers was complex. He condescended to Bridges, was politely enthusiastic about his friend Canon Dixon's patently mediocre work, despised Tennyson and Swinburne, and found among his contemporaries work of real interest only in the poems of the mildly eccentric William Barnes, who had called for a purification and reinvigoration of English through the use of compound words of Anglo-Saxon origin. Barnes came up with some evocative suggestions, such as *flameprint* for *photograph, faithheat* for *enthusiasm, outclear* for *elucidate,* and more than a trace of his ideas can be found in Hopkins's multiple epithets.

Among his predecessors in the tradition, Hopkins was fond of Anglo-Saxon and early Welsh poetry, as is evident in the elaborate alliteration in his own poems. He referred affectionately to Burns, although he found a "great want in his utterance," mentioned with respect Herbert, Spenser, Wordsworth, and Keats, but spoke with wholehearted admiration only of Shakespeare and Milton.

Perhaps the most illuminating statement Hopkins made about another poet was in 1882 when Bridges sent him a poem of Walt Whitman's, commenting on a resemblance between Whitman's poems and Hopkins's and inquiring whether there may have been some influence. Hopkins replied that he knew a half dozen or so of Whitman's poems and remarked on Whitman's "marked and original manner and way of thought and in particular of his rhythm." He then went on to say, "I always knew in my heart Walt Whitman's mind to be more like my own than any other man's living. As he is a great scoundrel this is not a pleasant confession." The rest of Hopkins's letter to Bridges consists of yet another explication of his own metrical innovations, comparing them this time to Whitman's. Sounding challenged by the only real competitor in sight, he tries to demonstrate that although Whitman's music is interesting, he is, unlike Hopkins, really only writing "rhythmic prose." "The above remarks are not meant to run down Whitman," he finally writes, as though coming to himself.

What, though, could Hopkins possibly have meant when he said he felt so much fellowship with Whitman? The American "savage," the self-appointed poetical and spiritual prophet of his country, yawping across its rooftops, and the withdrawn, pious, touchingly delicate and high-strung Jesuit priest!

And why, after proclaiming so much affinity with Whitman, would Hopkins have called him a "scoundrel"? Many of Hopkins's commentators have assumed that he was reffering to Whitman's by then much remarked upon homosexuality, which would presumably have threatened Hopkin's own suppressed sexual tendencies. But there is no reason to think that Hopkins would have rejected Whitman for such matters any more than he would have any of the many homosexuals in the large "bohemian" artistic and intellectual community he'd known in Oxford and London before he took his orders.

Both the sympathy and antipathy Hopkins felt toward Whitman had to have had deeper roots. I think what Hopkins would have been most struck with was the way Whitman's poems were so clearly informed by a coherent and systematic vision. Hopkins was fascinated by the evidences of vision he found in other poets, remarking it in Blake and in Wordsworth's intimation ode, and he would have immediately realized that he shared with Whitman a belief in the spiritually transforming power of poetry, in its redemptive faculty. The sensuality of Hopkins's imagination, the physical palpability of his cognition, were remarkably similar to Whitman's, but more importantly, both poets were driven by a conviction that the power of poetry goes beyond its aesthetic expressiveness, that it is potentially an implement of spiritual evolution.

Where the two poets differed was in their characterization of the spirit. Whitman was trying to create a poetical-metaphysical ground for the paradigmatically modern American experience. His poetry takes as its task a fundamental liberation of consciousness, and this liberation entails also a rejection of received forms of religion. Hopkins had to acknowledge the resonance Whitman's poetry rang from his own, but he would have been offended by this drive in Whitman toward a secularization of consciousness and would not have been able to offer much sympathy to a vision he probably believed was finally heretical, if not infernal.

Hopkins's own vision, just as radical in its rejection of received notions of rationality, and insisting on a similar transfiguration of sensibility, was still firmly grounded in his religious faith. Reading Whitman might have made Hopkins suspect that in his own poetry he was trying to make that faith serve a function for which it wasn't suitable. Hopkins took to heart the humility his religion asked of him. His willfulness toward himself and his muted claims for his poetry both partake of this humility, and if the focus and energy he manifested in his work implied a confidence, even an arrogance toward received forms of poetry, he could admit to none of the exuberant hubris in which Whitman so exulted.

Hopkins is firmly in the tradition of religious poetry in English. Although there is no evidence he knew Donne's work, which was almost totally neglected in the nineteenth century, his poems are like both Donne's and Herbert's in the way they serve at once as elements in a dialectic of faith and as acts of belief in themselves. But Hopkins differed from his great predecessors and was closer to Whitman in his modernist intuition that poetry could actively embody in and of itself ultimate realities.

His methods were his own. Taking cues from Ruskin, who had promulgated an obsessive attentiveness to the individual in the type—what Hopkins would famously call the "inscape" of things—Hopkins drove his sensibility and imagination to a state of almost ecstatic intensity, something close to a mystic's numinous union with reality. Whether Hopkins was actually a mystic is not the point: like the mystic, he forces his faith until it ceases to be passive and receptive and becomes dynamic, acquisitive. The poems recuperate faith, but go further by striving to include the very essence of metaphysical reality in their burning simultaneities.

Hopkins was asking something new of poetry; that his poetry would have seemed "odd," even to him, is hardly surprising. There must have been something vaguely sinful to him in the sensuality of his work, in its sheer voluptuousness. Not only faith, but cognition and intellect become sensualized in the poems, almost eroticized by their propulsive force. Hopkins pushed the music of his poems to the point at which their meaning began to disintegrate and urged their figuration to a density that had little to do with any traditional notion of expression, and everything to do with Hopkins's intuitions of a new genre of spiritual communion. Even the strained diction of the poems asks the reader to give over received notions of rightness, of reasonable and banal consciousness, for the potentially (and threateningly) miraculous. To experience Hopkins's poems fully doesn't demand interpretative ingenuity, but rather the willingness to surrender to their aesthetic and spiritual mysteries. The poems draw us into themselves on a level previous to the part of mind that normally wills itself through a poem; the language seems to partake of what modern psychology has called the primary process, the pure, unmediated language of the unconscious as it moves in a primitive sensuousness.

> I caught this morning morning's minion, king-
> dom of daylight's dáuphin, dapple-dáwn-drawn Falcon

"Ma, ma, ma; da, da, da, da, da, da . . ." The echo of the nursery and in the same gesture the astonishing movement by which the hawk of the air will be sublimated through the poem's hectic, charged figuration into a symbol of both religious consummation and a radically heightened perceptual awareness.

Hopkins said several times that he wanted his poems to be read with the "ear" rather than the "eye," but when we give ourselves to them wholeheartedly, we can feel as though we're reading, as we rarely do, with the entire body and with parts of the soul that usually stay uninvolved in such matters. Hopkins's poems attempt to release consciousness into a universe in which the natural is transfigured, not into a Rilkean "invisibility," but into a corporeal incarnation that will embody the greater realities beyond it. If Hopkins's poetry was an essential part of his religious undertaking, for us it brings to the tradition an exaltation in which "the world's splendour and wonder" becomes accessible in a way that is at once mysterious and profoundly inspiring.

Fearfulness and Will

The Poetry of Paul Zweig

"Afraid that I am not a poet . . ." Paul Zweig begins a poem in his first book, *Against Emptiness*. For some poets, the act of writing a poem is not the simple singing out of the overflowing soul common wisdom reports to us, so much as it is a test of character. The tensions implied in this trial have nothing to do with timidity, faintheartedness, or any of the many neuroses that can inflict the writer. They have instead to do with the poet's conception of the poem, with what the poem asks, of what he or she believes it is capable. Whether consciously or unconsciously, the poet commits to a kind of gamble that is based primarily in a largeness of ambition, in nearly impossible longings both for the poem and for the self. The poem demands more than verbal felicity, more than musical ingenuity, more than imagistic or metaphoric agility, because what the poet has in mind for it are matters of the spirit, questions of ultimate identity, of transcendence and exaltation. The self that might create such a poem is a creation, too, one that will make unusual and exacting demands.

Of all the intricate questions, literary, aesthetic, historical, and moral, that must be confronted before a poet can write a poem, the most subtle and the most difficult have to do with issues of spiritual identity. For the poet, as for anyone else, the great questions of existence have to do with the tensions between what there is in our characters to which we must resign ourselves and what we believe is perfectible, which requires our best energies for its sometimes very problematical realization. In

---

the poet, though, this struggle is intensified, because what the poet is trying to discover about the self, about strength and weakness of character, about the possibilities of the soul and about its limits is both the subject of the work and its medium. For the poet whose ambitions reach beyond the desire simply to generate verse, whose wishes for the self may not be congruent with general human aspirations but are focused instead on the difficult attempt at informing the ordinary with the transcendent, there are terrific risks. The subjects of poems, the themes of poems, are always in the process of moving beyond themselves: a poem of love can also be a poem of lust for mystical union, an homage to a family member can become an expression of the sad dissatisfactions the poet senses in ordinary perception and ordinary community.

Everything can seem to be at risk during the time of the poem: the spiritual condition of the poet, his or her personal past and future, the social and historical situation in which the poem is taking place, and, finally, the very right of the poet to attempt to compose the poem.

"Afraid that I am not a poet," the poem begins, but then goes on, "Yet willing to write / Even about that," thus expressing both the fearfulness involved in Zweig's conception of the poet's task and the courage that will be characteristic of his work throughout his poetic career. From the earliest poems, Zweig was involved with the kind of demanding spiritual conflict we find in the most adventurous literature. "Afraid that I am not a poet . . . " How to even begin, the poem seems to be saying, when there are such territories to be charted, such forbidding realms of self to be meditated? More rendingly, as the poet senses the ultimate dangers of these undertakings, the poem asks, "How can I be sane with borrowed faces?" But the undertaking is irrevocable now, the poetry is under way, the process, which will absorb the rest of Zweig's creative life, is wholly involving.

In Zweig's early poems, the existential obsessions of the work are often expressed in these sorts of direct questions, posed with an almost naïve obsessiveness: "What have you done to need life so badly?" ("The Natural History of Death"); "Where is the terror that rots under the shirt front?" (the same poem); "How can I escape the invisible father and mother?" ("America at War"). At first, the poet doesn't seem quite to understand the real import of his own projects. The questions the poems ask can seem plaintively off the point, as though the poet felt only a generalized unease, a quandary about his purpose. What will later become the precise substance of a desire for transcendence, for the comprehension of a reality beyond the quotidian, here is expressed with only the vaguest sense of the specificity of the poems' real possibilities. Often there is a somewhat nostalgic regret, the traditional romantic glancing back toward the past as though there, perhaps, the unity, the harmonies that existence promises, may already have been experienced, but with a consciousness not yet sufficient to recognize them. Even the most personal, intimate past is called into question, is made a part of the adventure of the poem. History itself becomes a variable in the struggle, as do religious and philosophical investigations and the genealogies of literary and artistic imagination. The poems struggle in their formulations: images occur, portions of reality swim in and out of significance, symbols take on resonance, are noted, but quickly lose their intensity and their efficacy. In the course of a single poem they are elaborated, exhausted, and sometimes even become the occasion for irony or self-mockery, because of their false or at least transitory illusoriness. But at the same time there are, always, in the core of the poems, beneath their apparent uncertainties and confusions, the rigorous demands Zweig would always require of himself, and of his work.

Later, in *Eternity's Woods,* the propositions of inquiry become more subtle, more complex, and still more demanding: "To exist at the highest level; / To be entirely conscious, so that even my smallest sigh / Glides happily, and the deathwatch is never bored" ("Stanzas in an Emergency"). The soul longs quite articulately here toward something beyond the din of relationship and of intellectual quest. The soul longs, and attempts, and fails, at least at first. Reality itself begins to be called into question, the very matrix of being, of self, the origins of self and the manifestations of self as they find form in the gentler elements of human possibility: love, companionship, family, the consolations of solitude. The issue is whether the poet will be able to continue to exist in the state of partial realization, partial consciousness, partial being that the poems manifestly are struggling against now. The drama of the poems often becomes entirely philosophical and spiritual. What the consciousness seems to be seeking now is unremitting progress, growth. The growth of the mind itself has risks, though, because as mind becomes more aware of its potentials, of its own awarenesses, and hence of its freedoms and responsibilities, it demands more of itself: there appear more assumptions of attainment, of improvement, of the possibilities that soul must entertain and attempt with the larger scope it has been offered. Also, with so much commitment to consciousness, dangers appear. The poems now clearly begin to confront the various inertias the world of reality holds for us, the delusions of attachment: all the genres of spiritual suppression a civilization with no apparent soul offers the besieged self; greed, hubris, intellectual satiety, and the sheer weariness the project of fulfillment entails.

Zweig offered his spirit to these uncertainties in a way that is rare in American poetry. His poetry from the beginning was driven by the questions he asked himself, and sometimes, in the dramatic energy with which he sought to answer them, along with the skepticism so natural to his mind, he almost seemed to become the victim of himself. This theme, in fact, comes up again and again in his poetry: the self riven by the difficult and uncertain needs of self, the self asking the apparently impossible from itself, and even the self that is as fragmentary as these fragmentary acts of imagination, the poems that somehow spring from it. The poems themselves, these miraculous but in some ways utterly unforeseeable productions of consciousness, were to be marveled at with gratitude and delight, but also with a sense of distrust. This delight and this distrust make for a dialectic in the very heart of the poems that is fascinating in the confrontations it entails.

In the poems written near the end of Zweig's life, the force of the tireless intellect that drove him to such rigorous questioning, and the generosity, sensitivity, and imaginativeness of his character fused and tempered these struggles. The very last poems, written in a frenzy of inspiration—as the death that he had lived with for six years and that was by now known and not known, dreaded and entirely engrossing, came ever closer— have a spontaneity, a purity, an energy, and a forthrightness that is nearly overwhelming. These astonishing songs, almost without traditional subject matter, are wide-ranging, far-seeing, and resolutely focused. It is as though all of existence itself, life and death themselves, had become certain as the object of the poems' task, and with this certainty of object came certainty of subject. The poet fused absolutely with his poems, becoming as large and high-minded as they were, with a clarity and an assurance of self that was a consummation of all the struggles and all the attempts and false attempts of a life of scrutiny and spiritual adventure.

Beginnings

1

When I graduated from college, I did what I imagine every would-be writer does: I sat down and tried to read everything I'd ever heard of. I read all of Homer, Shakespeare, Sophocles, and Aeschylus. Dante and Virgil, and of course *Paradise Lost,* which for one long week almost made a Christian of me. As much Blake as I could struggle through; some Chaucer; Whitman, who'd been the first poet I'd ever read voluntarily; Yeats, the poet I'd gone at most passionately while I was in school; Eliot, who was *the* poet then, especially in the academy, especially *The Waste Land,* or its footnotes. A lot of Stevens, some William Carlos Williams, although I didn't quite understand him yet—mostly I read *Paterson;* some Auden, Keats, Coleridge, not much Wordsworth, whose clarities deceived me, not enough Shelley, who seemed so longwinded; Donne, Herbert, even Traherne; Wyatt and Sidney, Marlowe, Webster, no Spenser, who was a perfect soporific, not much eighteenth century, which was the moon. There were many others—Crabbe and Meredith for starters—and probably many I've forgotten. I was also going at the novelists—almost all of Dostoyevsky and Tolstoy, Melville, Hawthorne, Conrad; most of Laurence Sterne, a lot of Faulkner, Hemingway; Joyce, except *Finnegan,* a little Dickens, who was so entertaining I found him suspect; less James, too stuffy; not many contemporaries, Bellow and Gaddis, and a little later and more thoroughly and gleefully Henry Miller. I struggled through what I could of the philosophers and social thinkers. Of

© C. K. Williams. First published in *In Praise of What Persists,* edited by Stephen Berg, 1983.

Not that I understand: he is something between a camera and a short-story writer — not really a poet.

the philosophers the Greeks mostly, mostly Plato; of the others a lot of Frazer and Jung, who were still having their vogue then. I once outlined, out of lord knows what forgotten good intention, the entire Tibetan *Book of the Dead,* and copied out in its entirety the *Mystic Gloom* of the Pseudo-Dionysus. It was all more or less nonstop: I'd fall asleep every night over a book, dreaming in other people's voices. In the morning I'd wake up and try, mostly fruitlessly, to write acceptable poems.

In memory, those years seem so distended, so grotesquely swollen with frustration, uncertainty, and loneliness. It wasn't until I actually stopped to count that I realized there were only four or five years, and not the greater part of my adult life, of what could most benignly be called my apprenticeship. Just learning to be alone was such a Heraklean task. The world always offered so many enticements. And, at my desk, how my mind would drift, how I'd tear at myself with doubts, with self-accusations—I was surely indolent, probably spiritually inept, trivial, inconsequential, not cut out at all for this; no gift, no discipline. That fractured image of myself became myself: I was just as unhappy as you were supposed to be, as all the stories had you be, which may have been all that kept me going, because I was so lost by then; I had no idea anymore of what I was doing, I had no notion of what a poem even was.

I knew that I was deeply committed to poetry, but I wasn't quite sure why and was very uneasy about it. I hardly read any contemporary poets at first, I didn't know any other poets, had no idea of how to find any, and the poems I did come across I usually dismissed as either incomprehensible or trivial. It's re-markable how young artists always seem to make and feel perfectly comfortable with such outrageous exaggerations. Right along with a wracking lack of confidence, you can proclaim to yourself that there's nothing around of any real value, nothing in sight, and nobody but you who has any notion of what's really going on or needed. All you're really trying to do is clear the slate enough to get your own scrawl on it, but all this struggling can be very aggressive, maybe because you often have then so much the sense of being put upon, oppressed, by just about everything. Because I was so alone in it, I think I may have been even more impressionable than the young poets I've met since. I was always coming to odd conclusions. Once I decided that the whole tradition of English poetry was useless to me, and for a few years I didn't read anything but translations. That was before the great age of translating that began in the middle sixties, and I must have inflicted an awful lot of wretched translationese on myself. I did, though, find Rilke and Baudelaire, who were terribly important to me, and Verlaine, Rimbaud, and Char; Montale and Seferis, the haiku poets, and Rexroth's Chinese and Japanese, mostly Tu Fu and Li Po. Really, what I read seemed to have been determined mostly just by what had been done, what I could get my hands on.

Ransacking other traditions that way, though, still didn't help me much in my own work. I was still frustrated, still mostly at loose ends and without direction. Then somewhere around that time I came to another odd conclusion, and made what seems to me now, considering how confused I was about most things, a surprisingly concrete and purposeful decision. It mostly had to do with all the work in longer forms I was reading, with how comfortable I felt with Homer or Dostoyevsky, and how ill at ease with contemporary poetry. I began to feel that a great deal of human interaction, a large portion of real moral sensibility and concern, had somehow been usurped from the poets by the novel and drama, and that in the face of it there had even been a further kind of protective withdrawal and a tunneling of vision on the poets' part. It felt to me as though anything that was on a large emotional scale, anything truly passionate, absorbing, or crucial, had been forsaken by poetry. What the poets of our time seemed to be left with were subtleties, hair-splittings, minute recordings of a delicate atmosphere. Even in the poetry I could find to admire for one technical reason or another, there seemed to be a meagerness of theme and attempt compared to the works in longer forms. I think my ideal as a poet then was Homer: I was fascinated by the sheer weight of the data, in the *Iliad* particularly, the utter factness of its human experiences, its absolute commitment to the given.

Oddly enough, the conclusion I drew from these reflections didn't send me to write novels or plays myself, certainly not epics. I was still, although I might have had a hard time saying why, absorbed in the lyric. I had, though, been writing some stories, I'd composed a play in college and assumed I would again, and had done some criticism—book reviews and reviews of art shows—for a local paper. Now I decided I wouldn't do any of that anymore. I resolved—the word applies; there was that much unexpected will to it—that anytime I had an idea for a story (I had notebooks of them) or for a dramatic sketch, or for anything resembling more purely intellectual activity—criticism, any sort of philosophizing—I'd try to find a way to get its matter into a poem.

It's hard to remember how long exactly it took me to come to what seemed like such an extreme notion; it's harder to remember what it felt like at the time. Surely all young poets flounder through similar crises and make as unlikely fusses; fortunately, we don't have to know that everyone else is doing it too. However little my decision may have actually affected the evolution of my work (that kind of thing would be hard to know really), it was certainly very important, primarily because beyond the vague sense it gave me of having a purpose now, a sort of goal, I was paradoxically able for the first time to begin to study other people's poems in a genuinely useful way: I needed them now, I wanted to see how aspects of my project might be being handled.

This all happened sometime between 1960 and 1965, and it's impressive to consider the books that appeared during those years that were important in any regard, and were astonishingly what I had been looking for. (That they incidentally made a joke out of my idea of the limitations of poetry went by me with hardly a flicker.) William Carlos Williams's *Pictures from Brueghel* came out in 1962 and was the key for me to the rest of his inspiring ahievement. Then there were Lowell's *Life Studies,* Roethke's *Far Field,* Berryman's *77 Dream Songs,* Plath's *Ariel,* Ginsberg's *Kaddish,* Merwin's *Moving Target,* James Wright's *The Branch Will Not Break,* Kinnell's *Flower Herding . . . ,* Bly's *Silence in the Snowy Fields* and the remarkable series of translations that he did himself or edited: Vallejo, Neruda, Hernández, Jiménez, Lorca, Trakl. They were all books that became crucial to me as soon as I stumbled across them, or as soon as one of the poets I'd begun by now to meet would direct me to them.

Now that I did know some other poets, it probably goes without saying that my project, my resolve, became even more of a secret than it had been before. I wasn't about to call that much attention to myself. Although I'd begun to write some poems that I wasn't completely ashamed of, I was still terribly shy and excruciatingly diffident about my situation as a poet. I still felt sheepish, for one thing, even guilty, about how I'd arrived at poetry. I'd never had that blazing calling our teachers had always indicated was the primary credential for it. Poets, we were given to understand, know who they are in the cradle: the rest is just a dechrysalization.

Poetry didn't find me, in the cradle or anywhere near it: I found it. I realized at some point—very late, it's always seemed—that I needed it, that it served a function for me—or someday would—however unclear that function may have been at first. I seemed to have started writing poetry before I'd read any. Although why this should have seemed to have been so much of a sin eludes me now, it reinforced the uneasy feeling that I'd had to create the interest in myself rather than having it dawn on me in some splendid conflagration. I'd always read a lot, but I wasn't particularly compelled by words for their own sake, or by "literature," which had always repelled me with its auras of mustiness and reverence. I detested almost any book I had to read, hated English in school, and I must have been surprised, maybe even a little put off, to find myself, just as the dreary poetry survey courses ended, turning the stuff out myself. I started writing one day, for no real reason (I had a girl who liked poetry, or liked the idea of me writing it anyway: not much of a clue), but once I did, I knew, I can't remember exactly how, that the realities poetry offered me differed in essential and splendid ways from those of every day. My everydays were all either tormented with confusions of one sort or another, or were intolerably humdrum. There was something about the way poetry isolated experience, its powers of demarcation, that promised a way to endow experience with forms that if nothing else would be at least more dramatically satisfying.

My first model as a poet wasn't even a poet, but an architect, Louis Kahn. I met Kahn just as he was becoming famous. My closest friend was a student of his, and he brought me to Kahn's office, a marvelously strewn muddle of rooms over a luncheonette. I liked Kahn and spent a few years in his circle. I think he enjoyed having a young poet in his entourage; he may also have liked having someone around who occasionally disagreed with him—his disciples never did—but I can't say that I studied with Kahn so much as that I studied *him*. I was fascinated to begin with by his notoriety: architects and critics were making pilgrimages to Philadelphia to see his buildings and to meet him. More to my real advantage, though, he thought aloud. He was a compulsive theorizer and lecturer, and it was an unusual opportunity to see how a mature artist approached his work. I'd had some inspiring teachers at Penn—Schuyler Cammann, the Orientalist, Maurice Johnson, my wry, wise adviser, and Morse Peckham, who to my great good fortune was developing then his system of close reading—but it was Kahn who without my quite remarking it formed most of my attitudes about art and the artist's task. He worked constantly, day and night. I was awed by that. Even more than his industry, though, it was what informed it that impressed me: the astonishing patience with which he confronted his work, the numbers of attempts he demanded of himself before he found a solution he would trust. He demanded a complexity in defining a problem, so that its necessities would always be as demanding as possible; the solution then was a purification, a refining to essentials, and his work always achieved a simplicity that belied what had gone into it.

It occurs to me that I've never really considered why, given all my admiration for Kahn, I didn't simply try to become an architect myself. It may have had to do with the fact that there were architects in my life at all. In some ways, for whatever obscure reasons of rebellion or reaction, I seem to have been looking for a sort of negative identity. I'd never, as I've said, met a poet, had no idea what one would be like, and I didn't particularly care. Not only was there no glamorous or heroic imagery to being one, there wasn't any imagery at all, and there must have been something about that lack of detail I found compelling. I'm still not sure why, but it feels as though I wanted to be something that *wasn't*. I wanted a way of being in the world without having to admit it. I was after marginality: I wanted to be at the edges of things, not quite really visible.

Such oblique needs. For a long time I fretted about it. Machado says somewhere that in order to write a poem you have to invent a poet to write it. You also, I think, have to invent a whole literature to receive it, and a whole community of poets who will have produced that literature. They'll all have biographies you've worked out for them, and I found after a while that my own biography had become as fluid as any of theirs. One's retrospective sensitivities and dramas can be absorbing—young poet being battered to splendid consciousness—but sooner or later reality recurs.

I think I had a normal enough childhood. Aside from the Depression miseries of never enough money, money battles at dinner, late at night when they thought you were asleep, it was mostly all right. My mother may have worried about us a bit more than most—her father and a sister had been killed in accidents—but she had, and still has, too much sheer joy in life to have let her cautiousness affect her much.

What I remember most from my childhood is how restless I always was, how hard it was to sit still. I always seemed to be trying to get away, out, from home, from school, from anywhere. I imagine I was just sharing in the general atmosphere of that war and postwar time. Things were moving fast then: it was the Boom, the "Rebirth of America." Coming out of the sad gray years of the war, there must have been so much promise in the air, so much hope.

It's odd. I realize I never heard during those years the word *hope* used in the sense I mean to give it here, not in our household anyway. Maybe because our hope, our ambition, our passion to advance, to move up, was so pervasive, so all-involving, that it never had to be mentioned, perhaps more urgently *couldn't* be mentioned, because expressing it might imply its opposites, doubt-in-hope and, unthinkable, loss of hope.

I didn't know at that age, naturally, how great a part of the population was rushing through those expansionist years with the same ambition, toward the same promise, and what an outlandish number of them were making it. Our fathers toiled their unbelievably long hours, drove themselves, worked like madmen. Our mothers abetted them, laboring themselves when they had to, at the store, on the kitchen table with the books. There was even something demanded of the children, something that, even if we didn't quite understand it, we knew was our duty. We were to have an *awareness* of it all, of our complicity in it. We were to be flexed, somehow, before it. Concentration, that's what it was. We were meant to *concentrate*. It was my father's favorite word in the little pep talks he'd offer me. *Concentrate!* Sometimes I felt terribly inadequate because I had no idea of how to go about it. That didn't matter, though. My father's lectures were very dear to me. What I took from them had to do more than anything else with his attentiveness, with how important he considered my outcomes to be. The seriousness with which he regarded how I was to project myself into my life probably was central to that general sense of tension and responsibility that came so early, but if at times it was inconvenient, I was mostly honored by it.

There were some kids, though, who amazingly didn't have it. We weren't all on the same flight after all, apparently. My friend Tommy's father was a fireman: Tommy was going to be one too. How relaxed he looks. I can see him strolling home from school, ambling, dawdling along. I never ambled: I ran, trotted, paced, counted steps, got there fast, faster, first, even when I was by myself.

Tommy was different in other ways too, it not so gradually dawned on me. His mother, for one thing, never let me in their house. A gang of us would be playing in back, the other kids would trail in for lemonade or whatever, and I'd somehow be deftly amputated from the group to wander off by myself. Richard's mother did the same thing, and Michael, one of my best school buddies, got me down one day and slapped my face until I'd admit that I'd killed God.

Small stories. It doesn't at this late date bear constructing any edifices on the relatively offhanded ethnic indignities of a Newark boyhood. Still, this business of being Jewish was complicated. The prejudice, overt or otherwise, was easy enough to incorporate into a part of one's personality where it wouldn't obtrude onto active reflection. ("Spit in my face, you Jewes," says Donne, me hardly blinking.) What I did notice with something that must have approached intellectual interest was that I seemed to have several histories. Everyone else did too, of course—Tommy was Irish, Michael Italian; they were both pugnacious enough about it—but they participated in a way I never quite did in the official history, the one we were taught at school, all those dates and names leading triumphantly to Christian Capitalist America. I don't know when I'd have noticed that that history and the one I was getting at *shul* had essentially nothing to do with each other. Very early, I know I'd squirm when we'd be exhorted by the principal—you still were then—to be "good Christians," but I already knew the advantages of expressionlessness, mild interest, mild boredom. There was such a discrepancy, though, between the two histories that I find it striking I never had any inclination to put them together, to collate them. They were perfectly distinct, and I left them that way: having two histories was as unremarkable as having two parents. I may even, on the imaginative level, have enjoyed it. Their narratives ran in opposite directions: the American one started in the present and reeled out backward, ending with the cavemen, whom I liked a lot, and the other one started at the beginning, which was a garden this time, and came this way.

That there were several gods, too, was beyond doubt. Michael, finally, after how many years of coyness, let me see his catechism. (It was exactly the same handy pocket size as the even more intriguing pornography he'd produce for me a few years later. Speak of influence! Whenever did language offer so much sheer glowing revelation as it did in that grubby, hand-typed samizdat of erotica that resolved so many burning questions of anatomy and mechanics?) The catechism, anyway, said, in cold print—yes, there it was—that the Jews *had* killed Christ, God, *that* God, a God I had to admit I found, despite the contentiousness of his adherents, not all that unsympathetic. Later, when I came back to it all, through Buber and Kierkegaard, and had my theodicy arguments with the God I created out of I-Thou and my Sickness unto Death, probably much of the energy for it arose from the possibility of there being a kind of Manichaean double to go along with that self-absorbed Lord of rapture and good intention. It may also have had to do with why in the poems I wrote for that theodicy, I mustered all the insistent Baalshem childishness I could to inform my queries and consternations. God as the path of accusation is famously self-limiting: that I kept it up as long as I did certainly had to do, too, with Michael's little book, the first one, that is.

2

To try to speak at all about the history of the poetry one has written feels redundant, because the work is so much the history of itself and seems to have implicit in it everything pressing I've thought about poetry over the years. What I remember most about those first days, when I was trying to give myself completely to poetry, is that while I wrote all the time, obsessively, painful, somehow I didn't really know what to write *about.*

I tried everything. In 1960, I took a job as the census-taker for the neighborhood where I lived; I think I was curious to see the inside of the buildings I passed every day, but without quite realizing, I may also have been looking for material. For awhile my reviewing of books and art exhibits at least gave me the semblance of the conviction that I could write something. Mostly, though, I just struggled, trying every imaginable kind of poem. Once I drove myself to compose an ode, rhymed, metered, unbearably mawkish and awkward, based on a sculpture group by Jacob Epstein at the Philadelphia Museum. (I didn't even have the good sense to have used Rodin's much better *Burghers of Calais,* which was there, too.) Then I wrote a sequence of about fifty sonnets about a visit to a prostitute, each with a different rhyme scheme, using half-rhymes and pararhymes (I'd been studying Wilfred Owen) and junked the whole thing.

It was simply one hopelessly bad poem after another. I knew the poems were bad, and although I did manage to write one that pleased me and that I published, a memory of childhood called "Sleeping Over," I was mostly lost, and terribly frustrated. I felt clearly—I'm not sure how I arrived at the notion—that I wanted my poetry to have an urgency about it, an ethical gravity: I wanted it to be about what was most important to me when I was most serious with myself, but I had no idea how to accomplish any of that.

When what I was looking for finally arrived, it came in a way I'd have never suspected. I'd been struggling on and off for four or five years on a poem about the Holocaust. I've written elsewhere (in the poems "Combat" and "Old Man") about the way the Holocaust was concealed from my generation of Jewish children: our parents never mentioned it in our hearing; they must have felt it was either too shattering or too shameful an experience to inflict on us. So when I first heard about it from an older friend around 1958, I was disbelieving, then stunned. "Six million dead," he said . . . and I hadn't even heard about it. I began to study the literature available on that awful massacre; I think I read everything that had been published in English until then on the subject, and I started compiling images, themes, and strategies for a poem about it. Anne Frank had already become an emblem of the Holocaust, though not so much perhaps as she was later, and I decided to use her as my primary symbol, with imagery and locutions from the biblical Song of Songs as a secondary resonance. "We have a little sister and she hath no breasts: what shall we do for our sister in the day when she shall be spoken for . . ." I worked on the poem very hard; it grew, it shrank, but I never could find a form or a music for it.

Then one afternoon I was reading an article by the novelist Thomas Williams about a trip he'd taken through the Southern states, about the fear and pain he'd had inflicted on him as a black man. This would have been around 1964; so much about the civil rights movement appeared hopeful then, and it seemed to me that Williams was being unnecessarily negative in his perceptions and conclusions. I started to write a letter to the editor, and to Williams, to explain why the situation for blacks in America wasn't as bad as Williams had made it sound, and from the depths of my political innocence I started to speak about the Holocaust experience to demonstrate why it wasn't. To my surprise, a few sentences into the letter, it suddenly came to me how wrong I was, that the black experience *was*, indeed, as bad as it seemed, worse than it seemed, and just as suddenly I was released into the Anne Frank poem: I heard its music, understood its structure, and in the next hour or two or day or two—I don't really remember—I wrote the poem.

I've said more than once to students and interviewers that I learned to write poetry when I was working on "A Day for Anne Frank," but I've never really made clear to myself what I mean when I say that. Thinking it through again, I realize there was something that happened to me as I tried to write that letter to Williams, something about the way I'd had to split myself from myself, the way I'd had to confront the falsity and self-forgiveness of my own attitudes, that had opened up a new way of thinking for me. Without understanding how, I'd created a method of composition for myself that, no matter what stylistic changes my work has gone through, has remained basic to the way I conceive poems. Having to balance two apparently contradictory ethical attitudes at the same time, having to realize the contingency of my own convictions, however apparently heartfelt they might be;

to confront them and force them to a more rigorous, more honest level; to make the poem, in a sense, a dialectical event even if the argument with myself precedes the poem itself—as it did in the Anne Frank poem—allowed me to bring the poems to a central position in relation to my own experience, my own sense of the struggle to be fully human. My poems have a double function for me: they are about consciousness, in a more or less direct way, and they're involved just as much with the social, moral world with which my consciousness is necessarily concerned.

Strange, not to have realized this until now; all I knew after the Anne Frank poem was that quite suddenly I seemed to be able to write the poems I wanted to write, in a way that satisfied me, that made the struggle with the matter and form and surface of the poems bearable, and, more to the point, purposeful.

3

Things didn't always go swimmingly after that, to say the least. After my second book, *I Am the Bitter Name,* at a time of particularly painful personal difficulties, a divorce, among other things, my poetry, or my faith in it, collapsed, I stopped writing altogether for a few months, then very tentatively started again. This time there was no resolution or decision, however naive. All I knew at first was that something was wrong, that the poems I'd been writing no longer had any interest for me, and that at least at first I had no idea of what kind of work I wanted to do next.

In the poems I had been working on, I'd been engrossed by varieties of disjunctive consciousness. I was trying to find ways to embody political and social realities by structuring and figuring poems in ways that went beyond apparent limits of logical connectiveness. Although I wouldn't use that nomenclature now, I was trying to bring the unconscious to bear on those issues. Among the poets who'd marked a direction that way, I was taken less by the Surrealists, who'd possibly gone farthest with it but who I felt were too playfully sure of themselves, than by those like Vallejo, Hernández, Mandelstam, and the anguished Rimbaud and Artaud, who were driven to the limits by their ethical sensitivities. I'd also been quite involved with Freud and the more eclectic psychoanalytic theories. I was particularly taken with what is called "primary process" language, the language of schizo-phrenia, a very concrete way of speaking that manifests an over-riding absorption in the gross emotional charge of symbols, and little concern with logical coherence, or "meaning." (Vallejo's *Trilce* is probably what would come closest to it in poetry.)

Morally, this way of speaking, or of assembling reality, seemed to me to relate very closely to what I felt was the cardinal intellec-tual sin, that of coming to moral conclusions. The consciousness we call "logical" works with systems of grammar and symbolic structure that presuppose conceptual conclusiveness, but obvi-ously our motivational apparatuses have little to do with the clarity those kinds of conclusiveness seemed to me to imply. The historical plague of conceptual fanaticism that drives humans to oppress or slaughter one another I believed had its roots in that kind of incomplete realization, and I had wanted to write poems and imply existences that subverted, or at least circumvented, it.

Why the poetry I'd evolved out of these issues should have suddenly become of such little interest to me is probably beyond recapturing; my life in general then was in disarray, but what-ever the reasons, unlike ten years before, when I'd analyzed my situation and thought I'd found a way to act on it, this time I groped. When I began to compose the poems I'd been looking for, I didn't even realize it. I wrote drafts of several of them, put them in a notebook, and forgot them until I came on them later during a reading, read one, and knew I had what I'd been looking for.

Trying to speak now of how I arrived at those poems is of course reconstruction, but I went through a similar procedure at the time as well, because when I did realize that I was under way in a poetry that interested me, I had to examine it to find a way to ground more surely my so-far intuitive notion of it. I had to describe to myself what I'd done, in order to be sure it was valid, and that I wanted to go on with it.

I'd been studying a lot of longer lyrics: Williams's "Aspho-del," Whitman, Akhmatova's "Requiem," Apollinaire's "Zone," Rimbaud's "Season in Hell," and Artaud's "Van Gogh," and I realized that I needed before anything else more space to oper-ate in. Secondly, and more importantly, I decided that the poems I'd been writing, and many of those I'd been reading, operated by using a sort of code, what I called a "rhetoric." Poets and sophisticated readers of poetry share a fluency in this rather arcane system. That lyric poetry is all but a cipher to those who aren't regular readers is a sometimes distressing given, but it bothered me that even those who could and did read poems seemed to do so with a consciousness that was so aware of itself as being in a unique, literary mode that what could really happen to them was severely limited. The reader came to the poem, moved into that special space off in a corner of consciousness for a time, and then resumed real life. Although I had no interest in making any sort of democratically motivated "simplification" of the poem, in making it more "accessible"—poetry is, and should be, a passionately complex experience—I felt that the elements of that complexity could become less specialized, less "poetic," than we were accustomed to.

Much poetry takes as its lyric stance a rather passive position in the world. The poet in the poem is primarily a perceiver, meditator, reflector, usually of sensations, states of being, conventionalized slices of reality. Most of life, though, happens to us in terms of events, or at least in anticipation of events, or reflections on them. Couldn't there be a way to deal more directly and intensely with genuine life stuff, with the crude, turbulent emotional storms in which even the most trivial of our experiences seem actually to be embedded? Not "narrative," which implies process, progress, denouement, possible release from tensions of expectation: the universe I found more interesting would reflect more clearly in tragedy, which is always reaching beyond its primary anecdotes toward the deterministic, mythic, consciousness that presumably precedes occurrence.

I wanted to continue to construct tight lyric poems, using the complex structures and systems of logic I'd been interested in before, but there was another problem here. That is, those "tight" lyrics generally work by what we call compression. Compression implies a rigorous and admirable elision of anything not essential to the movement and resolution of the poem, but I felt that compression had in fact often become a convention that worked primarily by hints, and by omission. Much of the material of normal emotional activity tended simply to be left out, or at best implied. I felt that in order to begin to get some of that material back into the poem, I'd have to make the surface of the poem more flexible, and more immediately germane to our more pressing life issues. What I came to feel was that I wanted the poem to happen to the reader without the reader's at first quite realizing it; I wanted it to become a part of the reader's felt life in a less willed way, and in order to do that, I came to think that the workings of the poem, its interior, all that offers us the purely aesthetic delights of poetry, its music, its language tensions, the patterns of figurative association we might call the subconscious of the poem, would have to happen in terms of that surface. A poem might be able to sacrifice a possibly crippling terseness without having to lose any of the nondecorative tensions and intensities that are primary definitions of the lyric.

It seemed clear to me that the odd sort of motions my new poems had were just what I needed to begin to handle all these diverse necessities. I'd been experimenting with prose poetry, as most of the poets I knew had, but I didn't feel much interest in a nonverse poetry. The opacity of verse, what we call its musicality, its tendency to call attention to language's potential as abstract sound, as a music that indicates a matrix beyond, or previous to, itself, was too compelling to me. At the same time, though, while I wanted my verse to continue to be grounded in the language of ordinary usage, or more precisely, ordinary usages, the rhythmical units I was using were more and more extended. I pushed them farther and after awhile found that I was working in a much longer line than I would have expected to. It was a line, though, that while still asserting itself as a generative verse element, seemed to be able to handle more comprehensively the sort of subjects I was interested in getting into the poems.

What those subjects are to be once the space is cleared for them is, needless to say, the most important question. Rather than influences, it might be more useful here to speak of assumptions, of what the historical, cultural, and spiritual axioms are that determine and define the poetic identity. Since the French and American revolutions, since Blake, Shelley, Goethe, Wordsworth, on through Whitman, Baudelaire, Rimbaud, Nietzsche, Yeats, Mandelstam, Eliot, Williams, to mention those who have meant most to me, the artist moves to the center of history, not as commentator or moralist, but as lyric participant, as the most exactly self-conscious enactor of secular and usually democratic aspiration. Art becomes not merely an instrument of ethical suasion or of delight, but is a redemptive resource in and of itself. Whitman defines it most self-consciously and perhaps with the greatest degree of premeditation: through the poem, he says, the very substance of our spiritual consciousness is to be redeemed; we are, finally, to become utterers ourselves, intimate and active participants in the universe of ecstatic awareness of *Leaves of Grass.*

Whether, at the end of our wretched, murderous century, and stumbling moreover into the mean, vindictive future of Reaganism, there is still enough hope on the planet to sustain such apparently exalted ambition is a difficult, possibly depressing question. If, though, the artist has had to assume a more humble, or at least a more canny stance, the absolute minimum demand we would still seem to have to make of ourselves is that we be what Eliot calls the "socially engaged personality." There are risks in this, the risks of hopelessness, of fanaticism, of despair, but beyond that, for the poet there is a special anxiety, that which has to do with what we could call the lyric gamble. Choosing to enact one's self in the first person implies a belief that the person so evoked will have a connection to reality in ways that are spiritually essential and productive, but in fact there is no way of knowing, no matter how scrupulously one tries to oversee one's solipsisms, that the matters one is struggling with aren't ultimately idiosyncratic, having little to do with issues of any moment. We have to presume that all poetry is written with great seriousness: there doesn't seem to be any way to *decide* to inform one's work with cultural or historical significance, and it doesn't take much in the face of all this to have the sense of one's own case, and sometimes even the case of poetry itself, being trivialized or deconsecrated by events.

More and more lately, although I still come across poets I didn't know, or didn't know well enough—Milosz, for example, or Ashbery or Seidel—and even some who for one reason or another I knew about but wasn't ready to hear—Elizabeth Bishop, most notably, who dawned late for me, but explosively—I find that influence mostly consists now of going back to those who have endured for me—Williams, Whitman, Donne, Yeats, Eliot, Rilke, Lowell, Homer, Shakespeare—and studying them again. What I want from them, and what I find, beyond the ever engrossing mysteries of technique, is a reinforcement of the faith that poetry continues to be essential to what is more precious in the human, and that the sometimes painful responsibilities the life of poetry demands are not only not specious, not a burden, but an opportunity.

On "From My Window" ✓✓

Usually my poems are very difficult for me to write. They seem to demand an enormous tension, or a series of tensions, usually over a period of months or years, before I can find what they were meaning to be and what form they were meant to take. Although when a poem is done, the work that went into it is always in some gratifying way reabsorbed into the concrete fact of its existence, my sense of composition is still generally one of strenuous willing. The few poems that come more easily, like "From My Window," are intriguing to me, mostly because the labor they demanded seemed to have more to do with what was actually going on in the poem than in the overcoming of all the various character lapses and lacks that constitute so much of the act of writing, but also because there always seems to be a great deal in them I wasn't quite aware of bringing about.

Although the generating event of "From My Window"—the two men in the street—had happened three or four years before, when the memory of it came to me, I knew immediately that there would be a poem in it; the working out of the poem was relatively easy, and very exciting. It was as though the poem was already there for me; its existence, that existence which can sometimes seem so tenuous, depending on so many problematical acts of inspiration, was already assured. I felt as though I was *in* the poem somehow, wandering through it. My task was simply to note and to record, and all that was demanded of me was enough patience and attentiveness to find the proper music and figurations for the poem. I even intuited very clearly (and very uncharacteristically) what its rate of disclosure would be. Every

© C. K. Williams. First published in *Singular Voices,* edited by Stephen Berg, published by Avon Books, 1985.

day I would wait for whatever segment was to be, not revealed, because revealed implies something hidden or obscure, but rather given to me. It seemed that everything in the poem was already available: all my mind's eye had to do was focus, in this direction, then in that. Although, in fact, most of the other details and events in the poem are fictitious, or were dug up out of notebooks and the drafts of failed poems, their place in the mechanism, once I came across them, would immediately be self-evident. [The men in the real-estate office, for instance, I found in something I'd tried (and am still trying) to write about wealth and love, and as soon as I had found them, it was as though they were already in the poem; all I had done was to glance up the street to notice them. My energy, instead of being devoted to searching for an element that would triangulate the exchanges between the veterans and the narrator, could go instead toward figuring those kabbalistic letters on the plate glass of their office, and to introducing into the poem, albeit in an ejaculation, divinity, that divinity which is always potential to our reflections.]

All this happened—the writing of the poem—quite a while ago, five years or so. In reflecting on work that old, one imagines there'll be surprises, but perhaps because the poem did come so readily, I'm struck again by how much there is in it I wasn't entirely conscious of putting there. I know I'd meant the poem to be about forgetfulness, about sublimation, evasion, repression, false gestures of transcendence, false faith, loss of hope, and, in a deeper sense, about hope itself. Most of these clearly have to do with our relationships with time, but when I was working on the poem I'm quite sure I wasn't aware, as I am in looking at it now, of how many of the incidents and details are enactments or embodiments of those relations. The seasons, first of all, and how uncannily, almost biologically aware we are in our discernment of them; the young jogger, trying already to outrun age and death; the surveyors who measure and record for us, because our common memory is not to be trusted for such serious business as dividing up the planet; the warehouse, a receptacle against the trials of time that has itself become a victim of time, converted to less noble uses; the "Legion"—the American Legion—that exercise in lost glory and an often fierce, vindictive, reactionary nostalgia. Even the fat on the paralytic's belly is an accumulation of his desperations, the friend's obsessive tramping in the night is the image of his, and that innocent figure eight, which figuratively becomes a segment of infinity-eternity, is possibly the symbol of our own.

If I don't remember quite how I came to all the detailing of the poem, nor even what made me recall that terribly tumbling wheelchair in the first place, I do remember very clearly what the impetus for writing the poem was. When I'd watched that morning from my study as the travail of the two men unfolded, I'd been very upset, taken aback, embarrassed for them, with that strangely acute unease we can feel for strangers who forget their lines, whose tragedies or griefs or rages flood over into our lives. As I watched it again, though, in my imagination now, most of that feeling was gone. There was very little perturbation; I felt detached instead, cool, professional. I was seeking and seeing auras, atmospheres. Then something shifted again and made me realize suddenly that what had been really crucial in my original response had somehow been coped with in my consciousness, de-dramatized, shriven of nearly all the discomfort I'd felt as it was happening. Furthermore, it was at that moment that I seemed to have to confront and to admit to myself that without my quite noticing, my experience of the whole Vietnam War had in some essential way also changed; it, too, had found a crease in my memory mechanisms; it no longer held for me the same rages of offended justice and rationality it had so recently.

But so what? Forgetfulness is one of the gods' most precious offerings to us. The war, after all, was over; there are certainly always examples enough to arouse our outrage at government's grim, obtuse intention to repeat its errors and its crimes. Why be so upset about letting that wretched war just go?

It had something to do for me with a deep sense of incompletion. Nothing had happened in the public world to redeem the war, to make it in any sense an effective sort of object lesson. We would have Iran, we would have El Salvador and Nicaragua, as we had had Korea and Guatemala, but there was no comfort in that, because I understood that each of them in its turn would erode into the same spiritless channels of meaninglessness and futility, and it felt to me then as though all the fervor and passion that we had experienced, we who'd been against the war, the liberals and the radicals and "bleeding hearts," had simply in the most insidious way trickled out, of history and of ourselves. [Remembering those two men now, the one whose very body was the literal repository of our history, the other who was linked by his uncertain gesture of charity to his friend, I felt terribly diminished, even frightened, because all of my accountings and recountings of those war days, all the furious resolution we all had felt had been as though cellularly obliterated, and it was made clear, as apparently it must be again and again, how limited our moral capacities really are, and, more, that this seems to be a basic fact of human consciousness, the arbitrariness by which our most intense realities are selected to abide or dissipate in the duration we inhabit.]

[There's something else in looking at the poem again that strikes me as something I hadn't considered as I was writing it; that is, how utterly impassive the narrator is, how much absolutely the observer, how immobile I am there as I watch. I did know as I was working the poem through that I had been in some confusing way a participant in the adventure of the two men, but I realize now that this impassivity was the very substance of my bond with them. There's an element of helplessness to my regard that seems to correlate exactly to the helplessness of the veteran as he falls and waits to be labored back into his chair. That impassivity and helplessness is, I think, the ironic symbol for me of the actual impotence of those of us who had fought against the war, and then stopped fighting, or stopped understanding what the fight had really been about as our inertias and indolence and personal preoccupations overtook us. We were afflicted in a moral sense with as maimed a capacity as the paralytic was in his partial body, and with as confused a notion of necessity as the friend's, whose devotion demands that he reduce himself in dissipation and dissolution]

[Much of this, I think, becomes nearly explicit when the friend looks up at me, impales me, it feels like now, with that stare or glare which may or may not be accusation but which at any rate has intensity enough in it, however inarticulate, to make me look away, to make me cast myself out of the time of the poem into another memory, into a past less menacing and less ethically demanding. A remembering that is forgetting. The poem first remembers the friend in his moment of despair or doubt, then looks away again, erasing him utterly, as though to obliterate utterly the demands he might be making of us.

It's that look of his that seems now to me to be the center of the poem, its fulcrum. It's almost as though an experiment had been taking place, and what happens to me, the observer, is that an element in my experiment suddenly makes clear that I am an element in *its*. The impassivity and apparent objectivity, which had seemed at worst mild curiosity, morally neutral, begin to resonate with implications of passivity instead of impassivity, inaction rather than objectivity, and even a withdrawal seems implied, a step back into that other system of omissions and disattentions that seem to be the content of so many of our lost imperatives.

It might be that much of our moral education consists in just such apparently minor, oblique encounters. The human mind seems to have no difficulty in spinning out grand systems of ideals and belief. We doggedly go about grounding ourselves in our metaphysics, in "greater" realms, but it is just this sort of confrontation that reveals to us how chancy and contingent those realms actually can be. Faced with someone else's pain, with the raw fact of another's reality, the epiphany always seems to be the same: that the other really does exist in his or her own right, and with exactly the same burning self-awareness that we do. A response is called for from this realization; what that response might be is uncertain, but one thing it has nothing to do with is pity. Pity implies a spiritual attention that might be optional. The urgencies of our encounters consist rather in the potential they have as responsibilities, in demanding of us that we go back into ourselves, to re-form ourselves, to resituate ourselves in a more self-conscious moral universe.

If there is hope to be found in "From My Window"—and I think there is—it would be in this. The poem finishes in its look away through time and memory, but perhaps that is because we have to look away before we can begin again. It is so daunting and exhausting to have to confront yet again those questions of accountability that are at the core of our spiritual dialectic. We seem to have to force ourselves again and again to try to reconcile the incongruities of our conscious life, the discrepancies between our intentions and our acts, the astonishing gap between our ability to elaborate admirable ideals and the ease with which we slip from identity to identity to evade them. Whatever hope we do have would seem to have to be found in ourselves, and in our awareness of those others who are the greater moral portion of ourselves.

From My Window

Spring: the first morning when that one true block of sweet,
  laminar, complex scent arrives
from somewhere west and I keep coming to lean on the sill,
  glorying in the end of the wretched winter.
The scabby-barked sycamores ringing the empty lot across
  the way are budded—I hadn't noticed—
and the thick spikes of the unlikely urban crocuses have al-
  ready broken the gritty soil.
Up the street, some surveyors with tripods are waving each
  other left and right the way they do.
A girl in a gym suit jogged by awhile ago, some kids passed,
  playing hooky, I imagine,
and now the paraplegic Vietnam vet who lives in a half-
  converted warehouse down the block
and the friend who stays with him and seems to help him out
  come weaving towards me,
their battered wheelchair lurching uncertainly from one
  edge of the sidewalk to the other.
I know where they're going—to the "Legion": once, when I
  was putting something out, they stopped,
both drunk that time, too, both reeking—it wasn't ten
  o'clock—and we chatted for a bit.
I don't know how they stay alive—on benefits most likely. I
  wonder if they're lovers?
They don't look it. Right now, in fact, they look a wreck,
  careening haphazardly along,
contriving, as they reach beneath me, to dip a wheel from the
  curb so that the chair skewers, teeters,
tips, and they both tumble, the one slowly, almost gracefully
  sliding in stages from his seat,
his expression hardly marking it, the other staggering over
  him, spinning heavily down,

to lie on the asphalt, his mouth working, his feet shoving weakly and fruitlessly against the curb.

In the storefront office on the corner, Reed and Son, Real Estate, have come to see the show.

Gazing through the golden letters of their name, they're not, at least, thank god, laughing.

Now the buddy, grabbing at a hydrant, gets himself erect and stands there for a moment, panting.

Now he has to lift the other one, who lies utterly still, a forearm shielding his eyes from the sun.

He hauls him partly upright, then hefts him almost all the way into the chair but a dangling foot

catches a support-plate, jerking everything around so that he has to put him down,

set the chair to rights and hoist him again and as he does he jerks the grimy jeans right off him.

No drawers, shrunken, blotchy thighs: under the thick, white coils of belly blubber,

the poor, blunt pud, tiny, terrified, retracted, is almost invisible in the sparse genital hair,

then his friend pulls his pants up, he slumps wholly back as though he were, at last, to be let be,

and the friend leans against the cyclone fence, suddenly staring up at me as though he'd known,

all along, that I was watching and I can't help wondering if he knows that in the winter, too,

I watched, the night he went out to the lot and walked, paced rather, almost ran, for how many hours.

It was snowing, the city in that holy silence, the last we have, when the storm takes hold,

and he was making patterns that I thought at first were circles then realized made a figure eight,

what must have been to him a perfect symmetry but which, from where I was, shivered, bent,

and lay on its side: a warped, unclear infinity, slowly, as the snow came faster, going out.

Over and over again, his head lowered to the task, he slogged the path he'd blazed,

but the race was lost, his prints were filling faster than he made them now and I looked away,

up across the skeletal trees to the tall center city buildings,
some, though it was midnight,
with all their offices still gleaming, their scarlet warning-
beacons signalling erratically
against the thickening flakes, their smoldering auras soften-
ing portions of the dim, milky sky.
In the morning, nothing: every trace of him effaced, all the
field pure white,
its surface glittering, the dawn, glancing from its glaze,
oblique, relentless, unadorned.

Contexts

An Essay on "Intentions"

I think that the primary business of poetry in our time—or at least poetry as I conceive it—is to offer evidence. We have to know what is there before us, we have to have the facts, and to get them straight, because without a clear and at least relatively detailed knowledge of our condition and the condition of our world, how can we expect to accomplish what are our obvious tasks: to confront, to cure or comfort, solace or succor, to change, correct, resolve, take into account, come to terms with, redeem, surmount, transfigure or transform? . . . How will we save ourselves and save this vulnerable world that so desperately needs to be protected from its protectors?

Because our capacity for blindness, for forgetfulness and for distortion is so limitless, we have to be reminded again and again of what is really in the world, or what is there before our eyes and what is within us—those double theaters offering us their tragedies and comedies, their grand guignol and slapstick—and we have to be recalled again and again to the difficult knowledge that not only are there two theaters, but that each of us is at once the tormented and exalted and valiant hero, the rapacious and licentious villain, and the spear-bearer in the dumb-show chorus, and that each of us is in some undeniable sense responsible for all the identities of all our fellows.

We have to know again and again what our tasks are and what

our capacities are, because despite our best intentions, and despite the fact that we all think we nobly and incessantly attempt all we can, we still manage to leave out so much, to omit so unconscionably much of what implores us or hints subtly to us of the necessity of our intervention. Our shortcomings, our unfulfilled potentials, our desires, acknowledged or agonizingly private, our ability to think like angels and to gibber like hyenas, the splendors of our ideals and the paucity of the means we have developed to implement these ideals, our overcomings and our capitulations, our willingness to confront our false fantasies and our weary wishes, and our submission to our incessant and erratic and wistful and impotent longings for something we are not and are not even able to specify very clearly—it is perhaps all of this that poetry must take into account now, and what is most astonishing, as always, is that poetry is not merely to offer evidence for all of this, but to *sing* that evidence.

It is within this apparent contradiction, this clearly unresolvable but ever-vibrant paradox that poetry exists. The poem, every poem, is to confront our two theaters, or our many theaters, or the endless bits of seemingly random information that flutter before us, and still do these two things at once: mean, and sing.

The language of poetry is narcissism itself. It calls attention to itself at every possible opportunity. It is as vain and self-conscious and as tensioned and competitive as an adolescent. It wishes all eyes to be on it: we are to hear its voice only, to love only it and to spurn its competition, although this competition is life, is everything else in reality, everything that has not yet been transfigured not only into language but into the particular language and the particular music of this poem. The language of the poem desires to be opaque: nothing is to pass through it. The subject is utterly incidental to it. We are to be conscious only of it, of its inexhaustible capacity for energy and play, of the delight it can offer even in the most dire recitation, of harmony and counterpoint, elegant association and brutal, lovely disjunction. And, further, in our age, in the epoch of the democratic, the language of poetry also wants us to know how it loves *us*: we are to be aware of how deeply poetry can delve into the language of our every speaking, thinking moment and still recover and display the poetry that is there, muffled in guises of function or of commerce or of chat. We are to know that we are musicians in our speech: our poems convince us that we are geniuses of music even in the most abashed recitations of ourselves.

The paradox of course is that at the same time the subject of the poem, whatever it is, flower or star, love or war or scrap of lost ambition, also makes clear and absolute demands. The subject is jealous of us: it, too, requires all of our attention, we are to bring upon it all that we possess: our language, our emotions, our most acute mental discrimination, even our passions, even our most banal experience; all is to be committed to doing justice to what is under consideration. The poem makes enormous demands: we are to be confronted with all our inattention, with how small mind we pay to what is offered us. We are to become aware of how little we have allowed experience actually to touch us, and at the same time we are to face the responsibilities implied in our awareness of that experience.

Consciousness by definition desires freedom for itself before all else, because consciousness by definition *is* freedom. But we also sadly know that consciousness has the uncanny and unpredictable gift of weaving veils before us, veils of habit, of inertia, of indolence and fear—there is even a veil of love that is the most touching of all. The poem is song and play and evidence, and the process of our interaction with it is also a stripping away of what is between ourselves and the realities that sorrow so for our engagement with them, and in this sense the language of the poem and even the poem itself seem to want not to exist at all. The poem is in the deepest sense to be a medium through which our attention flows, uncolored by any necessity whatsoever.

The essential mystery of poetry is that these two disparate elements, so contradictory, somehow intensify each other, when by any logical reasoning they should be distracting and subtracting from each other. Perhaps it is this paradox that makes poetry so forbidding, so "difficult" for many of the otherwise fine minds of our time. Or perhaps it is because poetry has assumed for itself—and all of us don't know this yet, don't understand what's at stake—many of the passions and concerns and quandaries that have traditionally been the realm of religion or moral or social philosophy, but which the withdrawal of God from our active affairs, or our exorcism of him, or our dedication to the realization of human promise, have redistributed through the continents of consciousness and of art. Or perhaps it is because at the same time that all this has occurred, the means of poetry, and the nature of poetry, have not changed and probably cannot and should not change very radically. Poetry is always being seduced to become what it is not: to be philosophy or fiction, theosophy or myth, but all of these quickly become mere means for the essential activity of poetry; they are means and moments, of no more urgency than anything else. There is that in the human which apparently always wishes to be what it is not: we are all in our souls young gods, dedicated only to what is most pure and profound in the universes of our existence, but if it is one thing that life actually and truly and undeceivedly teaches us it is that it is always the day to day, the lover's smile, the friend's death, the evident suffering of the stranger, or the scent of morning air, that determines who we really are in relation to everything else: to God, to our consciousness and our community, to the very notion of our essence. If poems are written that are not overtly committed to the quotidian, no poem can afford not to take it into account, and if those to whom poetry is a foreign language find that often it chooses apparently inconsequential strips of reality to brood or to reflect upon, poetry knows that this apparent inconsequence is not the question, it is rather our so-called deeper, or higher, or broader visions that are most susceptible to processes of selection, of abstraction, of generalization, of false raptures of transcendence.

In our moment, our terribly difficult historical moment, it seems as though our particular struggle is against how much of our public experience seems to consist of attempts to deceive us, to make what is evidence, what is there before us, have the consistency and contingency and mutability of dream. War is peace, terror is security, poverty is moral affront. Our politicians wish us to sleep and dream, the educational systems we submit to wish us to be functional, and what poetry offers us is a more acute awareness not only of this, but of everything, and it is an awareness that by its nature must be *felt,* with all the force of our being, not with mind or partial consciousness nor with a reprehensibly abstract pity.

Our poetry will paint the stripes on the tulip, this is its limitation and its glory, but as we paint the stripe we will also know and tell who owns the garden in which the tulip grows, and where the bulb came from and under what condition it was brought to us and who shovelled the manure upon its root and who picked and vased it on their shelf . . . and even perhaps what that room looks like and where the person who lives there is going out tonight, and how much they might know of all of this.

And we also probably have to know, we of the poem, how conscious that poem has been of *itself,* how much it has been forced to omit or elide, to avoid or evade or skip or skim because of the exigencies of structure or of form, or of that glorious song. For the form of the poem, and the quality and intensity of its song, is a part, and not a small part, of the evidence.

Of Poetry and Justice

In Euripides' tragedy *The Bacchae,* there's a curious moment. One of the focuses of the play is the band of women, the Bacchae, or Maenads, whom the god Dionysus has driven to ecstacy and madness and who have fled to the mountain Cithaeron. The episode I'm referring to concerns some men who tend cattle on the mountain, who come across the women and behold various miraculous, clearly supernatural happenings. The women weave snakes into their hair, suckle deer and wolves, and cause milk and honey to spurt from the earth. The men are awed, realize that they are surely in the presence of divinity, and yet when one of them suggests that they capture the women and bring them to the young king Pentheus so as to gain honor from him, they readily agree. There's no doubt that they know what they're doing is injudicious, that they are meddling with things beyond them, but they do it anyway: they attack the women and are put to flight, their cattle are destroyed and the women run amok, destroying a nearby village.

I have come to be fascinated by the speech, the quality of speech, of that one among the men who persuades the rest to act against their own best interests, for a reward of, at best, dubious promise. The messenger who relates the events—one of the cattlemen—refers to this other person as a wanderer, reports that he had lived in towns, where he'd learned, as I translate it, to "talk fast," and thus he was able to convince the others to undertake their rash action.

There's a similar episode near the beginning of *The Iliad,*

© C. K. Williams. Delivered as a talk at a conference entitled "The Writer and the World," at Northwestern University, 1985. First published in *TriQuarterly,* 1985.

when Agamemnon, inspired by a dream, means to stir his armies to greater ardor. The dream he reports to them is not the one that promised so much, but one he makes up, which seems to indicate that there is no hope for the Argives to conquer Troy, that they should, as he himself interprets it, cut their losses and go home. His soldiers are only too glad to comply: there's a general roar of relief and everyone heads for the ships. Agamemnon, though, has already plotted with the other generals, and Odysseus, in a surprisingly brief exhortation, cons the warriors into staying, convincing them that they are dishonoring themselves by thinking of their own mere mortality when there is triumph and glory to be gained, even though, as one of the common soldiers points out, the booty and riches of that triumph will actually go to Agamemnon and the other kings.

One last short example:

In his confessions, when St. Augustine is ruefully recounting the wild-oats days of his youth, at one point he says: "I fell in with a set of sensualists, men with glib tongues who ranted and had the snares of the devil in their mouths."

"The snares of the devil in their mouths." What is Augustine saying here? What is Agamemnon counting on in his duplicitous scheming? What is this "fast-talking" that Euripides recounts? In all these instances, there seems to be implied a special mode of speech, which is available to certain people. What that mode precisely is, is difficult to specify. Augustine gives no example of the persuasive power of his tempters. Neither the speech of Euripides' character nor that of Odysseus seems particularly eloquent. But it's clear that, in all these instances, the one who does have access to this way of speaking has an almost magical power of persuading others, of changing their minds, of convincing people to act against their own clear best interests.

We have seen, of course, a recent, and to many of us a particularly disturbing, instance of this phenomenon in the recent campaign and election. I don't think it is necessary to be radically partisan (although I fiercely am) to find the Reagan phenomenon at the very least mysterious, at the slightly less than very least, potentially sinister. The "Teflon presidency," yes, but the issues go much deeper, and our sense of disquiet, or of despair, should be much more acute.

What informs that despair, what we can find terribly upsetting, is the sheer power of Reagan's presence before the electorate. There *is* something magical in his speech, in just the terms I have meant to emblemize with my stories of the ancients. He is neither particularly eloquent, nor does he, according to surveys, offer a program that for most voters is particularly inspiring. Rather, there is something in the way he speaks himself, in the way he interprets reality for his listeners, that seems to nourish a hunger in the spirits of those who believe in him.

Historically, we know this isn't a rare circumstance. Perhaps the latest and certainly one of the most effective of this line of inspiring persuaders was the utterly banal, undersized, contemptible Hitler, who proposed a master race of creatures who were as unlike him in as many ways as possible, but who was received with the same sort of adoration and acceptance, and who maintained his eerie power over the German nation until it was in utter ruin.

It is the business of philosophers and psychologists, I suppose, to investigate this uncannily delusive and effective language, to analyze its efficacies and its victims' susceptibilities. As a poet, though, a poet with an extreme interest in the conflicts and paradoxes of our common life, I feel a deep and intimate sense of both menace and impotence when I consider all of this. For the poet, too, clearly has a special relationship to language. Traditionally, our mode of speaking has also been conceived of as approaching the magical or the mythical. When Plato banished the poets from his ideal state, he obviously had in mind our capacity for speaking in just such a potentially disruptive and compelling way to the youth of his Republic.

But it is unfortunately one of the continuing quandaries and struggles of the poet's life that although we know poetry is our most rigorous and most compelling mode of speech, as well as of action, for the most part it is as what we call "private citizens" that we find we actually can and do enter the public realm, as advocates, as organizers or as participants in movements and pressure groups.

I'd like, for a moment, to disregard all of this, though. Just for the time of this talk, I'd like to try to postulate a poetry that would actually fulfill Plato's prophecy about its potential effectiveness. Perhaps I, too, am being utopian, but I want to imagine a poetry that would indeed incorporate all the persuasive powers

Plato envisaged for it, while not ceasing to be poetry in a way that the poet can feel *is* poetry. I mean even to imagine a purely lyric poetry that would have this power of moral persuasiveness and social effectiveness. The reason I feel comfortable in making such an audacious program for poetry, even for the most innocuous lyric, is because I believe that many—most—poets, *do,* in reality, have in mind just such ends when they are composing their poems, and I believe it is really *all* poetry that can be defined this way. The very act of writing poetry is profoundly social, and beyond this, the consciousness that composing poetry presupposes in our age I believe also presupposes an awareness of the democratic vision that has been our opportunity and our responsibility since the French and American revolutions.

I do not believe there is or can be such a thing as an "innocuous" lyric, because the most delicate and apparently fragmentary poetic meditation must, sooner or later, come to consider its own basis, the soil, as it were, that nourishes it, in the self of the writer and in the wider social situation of that self. Poetry is, in its most profound definition, just exactly that relation between the most intimate self and the most public. The way we define the interaction has to do with how we define our poetry. The way we conceive of the private self as being in relation to the broader issues will determine for us the very music with which we speak, the image-world we will evoke for our readers, and the symbolic intensities by which we'll affect that reader. How directly or obliquely a poem deals with social or political issues is a large question, but the question is always rooted deep within the poet's psyche, in our most personal hope and love and terror; otherwise, what we are writing simply isn't poetry. The soul is not a creature living in a creature, isolated by walls of space from other creatures, but neither is it a kind of commandant of public reality, exclusively obsessed by larger issues, greater ideals, to which other individuals might be called upon to sacrifice their own precious individuality.

There's a term for the condition I am so awkwardly groping toward here, a condition in which the individual's passions and commitments, sense of intimate need and desire for spiritual and social progress are in an active relation. That term is *justice,* and it is in our consciousness of justice, that astonishing concept, that poetry can become the affective and essential agent poets intuitively understand it to be.

We have come, since the American Revolution, to misunderstand and even unwittingly to belittle the concept of justice. We have tended to equate it with liberty and the pursuit of happiness, as a part of that apparatus which represents for us freedom *from* various oppressive potentials in government, and in our fellow citizens. But justice is *not* a recitation of the Bill of Rights. As the Greeks conceived it, as the founding fathers of America envisaged it, as the great so-called Romantic poets dreamed it, justice is the human absolute, it is that which subsumes all the lesser categories. It is the active state of awareness of the individual participating in and bringing about the highest possibilities of human life in common, and of the human life in the individual, because these are inseparable. Justice is not, in this visionary sense, a public state of affairs, but a personal condition: it offers the human spirit its most passionate participation in common life, in common hope, in a contemplation of a society that is a process toward the moral perfection of every individual in that society.

I would offer, further, the notion that there is a positive and an active hunger within the soul for justice. I believe that once we are offered a vision of justice that includes the individual as the active and effective agent of his or her participation in that vision, there is no going back: we will henceforth, however inarticulately, suffer from that hunger.

It is my sense that the great historical paradox of our epoch, the age of revolution, the age of justice, is that those who manipulate us against our best interests and our best intentions, those who enact their malevolent magics on us, work through just this hunger, and this need. I believe that the efficacy of the diabolical Hitler and the incompetent Reagan is in their offering us simulacra of a vision that the spirit craves and needs, not for economic well-being, not for our securities and our fear of neighbors, but for that inward sense we have that human life, the human adventure, offers more than is being delivered, offers just this promise—justice—which is so demanding and so elusive.

Poetry cannot offer such false gods. Because poetry must arise from and be received in the most intimate places of the soul, it cannot lie in its speaking, nor can it speak at all without a general vision of the flow between the public and the private that is our spiritual adventure. The reason Plato banished the poets wasn't because he didn't like our singing, it was because we cannot not tell the truth in what we see, because the way we speak is truth, and because expediency and a petrified vision of soul, however apparently benign, cannot withstand the dialectic of the poem: that dialectic is the dialectic of the self and the soul, both of the individual and the community.

I do not know exactly what we will offer America and the world in its coming crises. I do know, though, that our poetry must offer, or rather continue to offer, a positive vision of that larger conception of justice which is our grandest political heritage. We must not despair for the susceptibility of the human to be deceived and deluded, but we must rededicate, redefine, and rearticulate our basic ideals.

That is clearly not *all* we can do, as poets and as citizens, in this difficult time, but it is the very least.

Admiration of Form

Reflections on Poetry and the Novel

Some of my best friends are novelists.

The "but," the "however," the slightly negative tang of re-
pressed prejudice insinuated in that locution are intentional,
though not any of its implied condescension. I don't intend this
to be a polemic against the novel, nor do I wish to set up an
adversarial relation between poetry and the novel. The novel
has enough enemies, and it would be foolish for a poet not to
realize that the novel's detractors are usually also those to whom
poetry, or any other product of the imagination, has little value
either. What I do intend is to question the overwhelmingly pre-
dominant position the novel and its narrative relations, film and
television, occupy in contemporary experience. If I mean to
suggest anything, it would have to do with the possible reestab-
lishment in our aesthetic consciousness of some of the more
formal modes of literary experience, of poetry in particular; I
want to propose that as a culture we reacquire the custom of
reading poetry as a complement to our currently exclusive and
possibly disabling immersion in novelistic ways of experiencing
and understanding ourselves.

Some of my best friends *are* novelists. There's a unique plea-
sure in going through the fictions of someone whose life you
know well. Reading becomes an intimate exercise of affection.
Beholding your friend weaving characters out of his or her
imagination, hearing voices you've never heard being generated
out of voices you know, glimpsing how these characters and

© C. K. Williams. First published in *The American Poetry Review* and *Brick,*
1995.

voices mingle with those of your friend, sometimes illuminating them, sometimes hinting at satisfactions or regrets you never suspected: all this is a very privileged way of being informed about another human being, and about yourself, your own assumptions and illusions.

Recently, though, I've noticed that reading novels *not* written by my friends is no longer as important a part of my life as it used to be. Although there are exceptions, books that for one reason or another seem to bring something essential to our tradition, I find I rarely seem to have time to read novels, or, with those that come to me so strongly recommended that I feel compelled to make the time, I'm impatient as I read, often a little inattentive, easily distracted.

I've been puzzled by this. I've thought sometimes that perhaps I've let my envy of the novelists get too strong a hold on me. After all, poets do have reasons to be jealous when we contemplate novelists' much larger audiences and much fatter royalty checks. But I've come to feel there's something more significant in my disaffection from the novel.

Like most people in our culture, I have to recognize that novels have been an essential part of my literary and moral education. As Lionel Trilling put it: "My conception of what is interesting and problematical in life, of what reality consists in and what makes for illusion, of what must be held and what let go, was derived primarily from novelists." And novels have also been involved in a very vivid way in my own biography. How forget sitting up all night for the first time with a novel—*Lord Jim*—and rubbing my eyes in the exotic Conradian dawn? Or that bleak, desperate February when I read all of Dostoyevsky I could find in English, and fell asleep every night over one of his books so that my dreams became an amalgam of his fictions and my anguish, the shapes of his characters' trials fusing with mine; I spent hours and then days as Raskolnikov, and then, to my relief, was no longer him, although he had been incorporated into me in a way I knew was important.

But now, as I say, I find I come to the novel less and less often. I used to fancy that someday when I'd retired a little from the world and had all the time I wanted, I'd finally get around to reading all the novels I'd missed, the Austens and the Eliots and the Richardsons, beside all the contemporaries who'd seemed to be worth reading but whom I'd never gotten around to. Lately, though, I've begun to realize that even if I ever did arrive at that dream of an endlessly expansible reading time, I'd probably reread, as I already do, Homer and Dante and Shakespeare, Herbert and Donne, and Keats and Yeats and Lowell and Bishop and Rilke, besides all my contemporaries who are fascinating and wonderful poets.

There are times, of course, when I don't seem to be able to read poetry, either. When this happens, my first thought is usually to put it down to fatigue: reading poetry requires an energy that sometimes can be daunting. But this can't be the reason I don't then turn to a novel. The narrative of the novel used to serve me as a distraction from tiredness, even from indolence: I could always pick up a novel, sink happily into that comforting storytelling, and feel as though I was involved in a virtuous activity.

The human mind seems to have an all but insatiable hunger for narrative. From the bedtime stories of our childhood, to our reflexive attachment to our daily papers, to our mindless consumption of the worst trash on television, we're driven by what seems to be a relentless compulsion to consume narrative discourse. How much of our lives we spend offering narrative to one another. Although to be called a gossip in our culture is a serious insult, in fact we are all gossips to one extent or another. *Real* gossips are those whose narrative need is more pathological than ours; what's most annoying about them isn't that they talk too much, but that they listen too well: they devour narrative so voraciously that we find ourselves recounting stories to them we had no wish to, as though their swollen narrative attentiveness in itself could overcome our resolution to keep secrets.

How much of our self-consciousness consists of the stories we tell ourselves about ourselves. Our education for the most part consists of the narratives by which our culture wishes to identify itself. We *are* our stories, or so we believe. To be narratively dysfunctional, to be unable to recite one's own stories, to other people or oneself, or to tell self-stories that are self-destructive, requires the attention of specialists trained in narration, psychologists and psychiatrists, who teach us to tell ourselves our stories more accurately, or gratifyingly, while at the same time also teaching us one of the key lessons of our time, which is to detach our narratives from any disturbing eschatological implications.

But perhaps there is a limit to our narrative hunger. As I've said, the novel has lost a meaning it once had, at least for me; I only rarely feel I'm being educated, or spiritually enlarged by a novel. I've even felt sometimes that the reading of a novel or watching of a film isn't somehow to be trusted. There are moments in fact when I feel I'm actually being discouraged, rather than exalted by prose fiction.

Of what might that discouragement consist? Surely many contemporary novels are, at least on their surface, saddening. Again, although there are clear exceptions, the characters in most of even our best novels are generally trapped in frustrating, sterile, spiritually hopeless situations. Almost always, the only way these characters can conceive of changing themselves is by changing their life situations, although they usually sense with foreboding that any new situation will likely be as hopeless as the one in which they're already stuck. The past usually exists for these characters primarily as a means of explaining the nameless anguish of the present, and the future often seems more of a reproach, a vague, wistful longing than anything else.

Another way of putting this would be to say that the characters of the generic contemporary novel are almost entirely lacking in what we might call a vision. The author ordinarily claims no personal vision either, although the reader is often made to sense that there may have once been a vision that infused either the author or one of his or her characters, but it has been lost, or violated, to such a degree that things may actually be worse than if there had never been one.

What do I mean by vision? I don't wish to imply any especially religious context by the word. Whether we have or don't have religious conviction and inspiration is a matter of how we interpret our place in history; it implies a kind of vision, but one of a different nature. What I mean by vision, put most simply, is the belief in the possibility of a kind of *radiance* in life, a radiance that, beyond all social and interpersonal insufficiencies, posits the ability to exist at least for some moments in a state of beauty: to participate wholly in the realm of the formally beautiful. Although this realm shares in the human soul many of the emotions of any spiritual phenomenon, it neither implies nor needs any genre of spiritual reality beyond itself; it is defined by an amplitude that asks for nothing beyond itself to redeem the inadequacies of ordinary life, and the incompletions and dissatisfaction of our metaphysical aspiration.

In literature, our most efficient, though certainly not our only access to this realm of beauty is through form, particularly form as it is manifested in poetry.

When I speak of "formal" literary experiences, I refer to those works that are defined by their involvement with and dedication to form, to the artificial conventions that generate form, and whose effectiveness and success can be measured by the elegance and ingenuity by which they satisfy those conventions without sacrificing either their expressiveness or their ambition for truth.

The conventions that determine form in art are often arbitrary. They are sometimes arrived at in a dialectic with the nature of their own materials, as in architecture, but more often their necessities are cultural agreements that only marginally have anything to do with anything tangibly essential. Thus music, which divides our aural world into a certain number of tones, then into rather primitive ways of organizing these tones—modes—then into various structural systems, such as the sonata or the symphony, which layer still more necessities onto the individual piece of music.

In poetry, formal necessities occur in terms of the movement of the language in its relation to more or less limiting metrical necessities, and then in larger structures of line and stanza, and the various formal organizations such as sonnet, sestina, and the broader conventions, such as elegy, or pastoral. The important thing about form, though, is its artificiality. In English poetry, the historically dominant iambic foot is closely related to the actual movement of the voice in our language between stressed and unstressed syllables, but the regularity of the iambic line, and the five beats of the pentameter, for instance, are purely conventional. In irregular, or "free" verse, where the cadences are not regular, and not counted, it is what Galway Kinnell has called the "rhythmic surge" that defines and controls the movement of language across its grid of artifice; the line in free verse becomes a much more defining factor of formal organization than in more arithmetical verse-traditions.

The crucial thing about form is that its necessities, though they are conventions, precede in importance the expressive or analytic demands of the work. Although a poem may to a greater or lesser degree seem to be driven by its content, in fact *all* the decisions a poet makes about a work finally have to be made in reference to the conventions that have been accepted as defining the formal nature of that work. If a compelling experience is conveyed in a verse drama, if an interesting philosophical speculation occurs in a lyric poem, if a poem involves itself in an intricate and apparently entirely engrossing narrative adventure, these are secondary, although simultaneous with, the formal commitments of the work. Experience must be embodied within the terms of those commitments, although finally these almost playful conventions, whether the structures of a musical mode or the pulse of a poetic line, will mysteriously intensify the emotion and meaning the work evokes. (I should mention, perhaps, that the dour and puritanical and ferociously self-serving "new formalism" has nothing to do with the definition of form I am elaborating here. The new formalism is rather a kind of conceptual primitivism that seems to gather most of its propulsive force from a distorted and jealous vision of the literary marketplace; it calls for a return to the good old safe and easily accounted for systems of verse, with counted meters, rhyme, and so forth. All despite the generation over the last few centuries, from Smart to Blake through Whitman and countless others, of an enormous amount of significant poetry in nontraditional forms; and despite the fact that many verse systems in the world require neither rhyme nor strictly counted meter, and despite the practice of many modern poets, who have been quite content to use whatever verse form fitted the poem they were composing. One would not want to sacrifice to such polemical excess either Rilke's free-verse *Duino Elegies* nor Lowell's *Life Studies,* to mention just two poets who worked in both systems.)

In the sense I am using the term, then, although the novel is a genre, it is not a form. The protocols the novel imposes on itself are too broad, too inclusive, and too indefinite. A novel or short story must have *style;* style can be, like Chekhov's, of such purity and moral inclusiveness as to be inspiring; so intellectually self-conscious and complex, as in the later James, as to make us wish there were another term to describe such intricacy and willfulness; and so ingenious and abundant, as in Joyce or Faulkner, as to leave us nearly breathless. But style—which a poem, not incidentally, must manifest as well—is not form.

It might be said that the novel is a shape, a space in which narrative can occur. This has surely been one of the virtues of the novel; it has given the novelistic project a discursive scope that in some instances can certainly be characterized as visionary, but still, regarded from the point of view of formal beauty, the novel is limited, by its very nature deficient.

A novel can manifest for us the undeniable grace of language being elegantly functional; novelists can write beautifully, and sometimes the grand word *poetic* will be wrongly applied to them, usually to describe heavily adjectival and figurative landscape descriptions. As I have already remarked, the novel is an undeniably keen instrument of moral reflection and can teach us a great deal about our dealings with others and with ourselves; it can serve as a forceful ethnographic resource, acquainting us with cultures and parts of our own culture that we wouldn't otherwise know. But novels differ from the more formal kinds of literature in that the movement of their language, however deft and dense, is driven to the utmost degree by the force of their subject matter, and only very rarely can a novel bring us to the condition in which we experience the radiance accessible to us in the presence of beauty as we feel it in the formal arts, such as poetry or music.

I don't wish to try to propose a theory of beauty; maybe I don't have one, maybe theories of beauties are contradictions in terms. Unfortunately the word *beauty* is often used in other senses, but I want to give it one specific definition here: as the product of a successful union of the formal and expressive, between the conventions of an art, and the human content the work of art encompasses and enacts. What we call the beauty of a person, or the beauty of nature, or the beauty of a scientific solution, are other phenomena. When we consider nature, in itself, and sigh for it and call it beautiful, we are distorting it into something that reflects our sentiments, but that has nothing to do with nature. Nature in itself knows and can know nothing of the self-conscious demands of beauty. There is nothing in nature that has this quality of imposing on itself artificial, arbitrary necessity, and then finding unanticipated delight in the working out of this necessity. Everything else in the realities we know submits in one way or another to external need; only beauty exists absolutely for its own sake, for reasons that have nothing to do with the purposes and requisites of human existence. Even our metaphysics, our cherished spiritual cosmologies, our religions, deal ultimately in this sense with the limitations of the human soul; even at their most exalted, they are what we *need,* to situate ourselves and our moral quandaries in our universe, and to ground that universe in obligations that point beyond ourselves. They are what we have to help us confront death, but beauty is what we have when we attempt to find our absolute definition of ourselves as living human beings. Only humans generate form, and only humans appreciate beauty for its own sake: what distinguishes the human from the nonhuman has to do with the unnecessary, the undetermined, the superfluous; all the characteristics of the beauty that arises from the logically absurd interactions of necessity and convention. And it is the lack of beauty in our lives that serves to warn us that we are being complacent about our experience, numb to our metaphysical hopes and limitations, and reflexive in our moral duties.

Of course there are other manifestations of form and its energies and consolations in human life besides beauty. In the traditional, more metaphysically grounded cultures of our past, cultures in which religious belief and commitment to ritual and ceremony still determined the actual shape of a human life, the narrative of a individual's experience was less crucial than participating in formal events that gave existence its ultimate meaning. Birth and coming-of-age rites, marriages and funerary ceremonies marked the shorter term of earthly existence; and the religiously defined, calendar-determined days of repetition and renewal were a reminder of human connection to realities beyond, and shaped the turning of years. These forms marked existence, they organized time and memory and meaning, and served to instill in the mind a capacity for intercourse with symbolic realities; they also were often put into opposition to the ordinary narratives of life.

Most of us have lost the capacity to involve ourselves wholeheartedly in the psychic commitment these sorts of formal ritual entail. Even if we feel ourselves to be religiously committed, for the most part we still participate in an essentially secular universe, in which rituals are usually occasions for social commerce rather than spiritual renewal. We don't generally feel we've lost anything in this shift: on the contrary, we have felt it to be a liberation from the conservative, constraining traditions that in the past made our mental lives seem blinkered and dark, and compelled thought and feeling in ways that seemed to have frustrated our capacity for both individual and communal meaning.

I'm not sure I, or anyone I know, can really describe what a more formal sense of life would be like. Not on an emotional level, at least, a level at which we can presume it was once lived in societies in which formal ways of consciousness were available to anyone, not merely to specialists, "technicians of the sacred," as Jerome Rothenberg has called the priests and poets who generate and manipulate symbolic forms for their societies. In our culture, there are nodes of people who live according to fierce religious convictions, passionate fundamentalist sects of every imaginable configuration, but they all, without exception, perform an elemental *rejection* of the common culture of educated people: sometimes it can seem that an irritable rejection of secular enlightenment is the primary movement of their spiritual activity.

For the rest of us, our experience of form, of a formal sense of life, if it is to happen at all, will probably occur in our relations with art. As Malraux pointed out in *The Voices of Silence,* our arts have already manifested a consciousness of this shift. The basic function of art in the nineteenth and twentieth centuries has enlarged to incorporate an elemental spiritual dialectic in a way it had not for many centuries, possibly not since the Greeks. It was a Greek, Euripides, who first perceived how painful, and possibly even fatal, the schism could be that separated the analytic, philosophically legalistic consciousness from the world of ritual form, which was once the matrix of ordinary existence.

We, rather than having our lives shaped except in the most incidental way by ritual and belief, have arrived at a situation in which we believe our lives are ours to construct as we please; we believe we are, and I think in the most profound sense of the term we truly are, "self-made." Our consciousness through most of the crucial moments of our lives is involved precisely with this creation of our identities, the refinement of our natures, and we are exquisitely aware of the responsibility toward ourselves this activity entails. The benefits of formal belief, ritual, and ceremony are forbidden to us except, as I've said, in our doings with art, and we have limited ourselves—which is one of the points of this essay—to a strongly diminished notion of art, as well.

This is the universe in which the novel exists, which it embodies, and which it addresses. Whether it is in the struggles of Dostoyevsky's characters with their metaphysical desolation, or in the soaring aesthetic ambitions of Joyce's Daedelus, or the groping of Roth's or Bellow's lost souls, the characters of nearly all novels are aware of themselves as involved primarily in the creation of their own characters and destinies: their lives are the raw material from which something is to be made, well or ill, and the most essential activity of life is just that making.

Usually we believe that the novel in this regard reflects certain historical tendencies: the rise of mercantilism and of industrialism, the development of democratic cultures in which the individual has both more value and more responsibility, have given rise to a sense of life in which the individual is marginalized and often in a state of despair about the difficult confusion between opportunity and duty, and the apparently irreconcilable struggle between the powerful and the helpless.

I wonder, though, whether the novel, rather than being a reflection of larger historical forces, might be a much more *causative* element than we generally think in these often painful attitudes. I wonder whether it might be that our several centuries with the novel as the predominant artistic experience have instilled in us a much more painfully narrative sense of ourselves than we realize? Might we without quite realizing it actually have what could be called a *novelistic* sense of life?

Might the novel, along with its capacities for edification, also inculcate in us an unconscious belief that human life is a closed narrative, a narrative we are in the process of generating ourselves, and that any direct relations with beauty we manage to become involved with are incidental to the grander narrative shape we imagine encompasses them, as it encompasses everything else? I think this is so, I think that without quite realizing it, and without quite being sure of what it implies, we have become, to the exclusion of nearly all else, the telling of our own story. We are to ourselves, in our essential definition, the novel of our own lives. And we have not adequately examined the implications of living in such a way; and neither might we fully realize exactly what the demands of shaping our narratives are, what perils might be involved in creating these life-novels.

In the world of the archetypical novel, characters seem terrifically free to move about as they like; they flow through a time that has no particular necessity, and that allows them to move about in any way they like so as to best go about their task of self-making. Most basically, the characters' narrative fate is always irrevocably determined by *events,* not by participation in any formal or symbolic reality beyond those events. The "meaning" of a character is revealed, and the "success" of his or her adventure, in the light of these events, whether internal or external. Redemption, or even resolution, if there is to be anything worthy of such grandiose categories, has to occur in terms of what has happened to the character, and what can possibly happen in the future. Furthermore, any event, present or future, has the potential to revise in a radical way the vision we have of a character, and which the character has of him or herself. In the harshest interpretation, each event has the potential for definitively convincing us that the character has "won," or "lost," and the character also will either have this sense, or if not, will leave us with the feeling that there has been a sacrifice of self-awareness to ward off its realization.

In most contemporary novels, the characters seem exquisitely conscious of all this, of the fact that any event can violently transform their outcome, and forever alter the quality not only of their drama, but of their own self-valuation. These explorers of their own destinies move through their lives with hesitation, tentativeness, timidity, and a passionate aversion to a too intense involvement in what they are doing or undergoing. They are aware in a frightening way of the potential for *losing* the narrative gamble of their lives. Any pleasure or joy they feel will usually have to do with their effectiveness, their sense of power, their ability to salvage moments of stillness from the terrible turbulence of this struggle. But the moments will be just that: tenuous, uncertain, immediately susceptible to the next turn of fate.

In most novels the loss characters experience or imagine they will experience is not the loss we know in tragedy, in which people are driven by a fate beyond the limits by which social entities can sustain them; tragic characters will continue to be, for the spectator, for us, redeemed by the formal intensities of the art of tragedy itself. Tragedy speaks of the uniqueness of the tragic hero's destiny; the novel speaks of the loss to which we all are implicitly at risk in the project of our self-making, a loss that will come upon us if our energy or attention flags, if forces of narrative shapelessness and meaninglessness are allowed to engulf us. We might almost say that the novel is an instrument of insecurity; its theme is quite often what may literally be taken away from us—love, money, our position in the world, a positive sense of ourselves.

Often this insecurity is expressed by an actual or potential exile. The uncertainty most protagonists in novels feel has much to do with their terror of being outcast, alone, or with their actually being rejected and alone. This is clearly another danger in the project of self-making: that the only way the self might be able to maintain its integrity is on its own absolute terms, and this might very well entail a metaphysical solipsism that excludes any other person's own self-defining. Over the course of the novel's evolution, there seems to have been an intensification of this sense of the protagonist's solitude. In most contemporary novels, the hero is terribly solitary. While Richardson's and Stern's characters moved through tight-knit, if intricate, social situations, which required a nimble sense of civilization to survive, and while Dickens's were painfully aware of the alienation that might await them at the margins of society, contemporary protagonists are almost defined by their solitude; they typically feel alone even in the most intimate circumstance, among family and friends, and even in the company of their own consciousness. The terrors of exile, of being cast out, which threatened many Greek tragic heroes, has become the perpetual condition of the contemporary novelistic character. This condition has often been blamed on the "alienation," social and economic, of the individual in modern society, but again, the way the novel has shaped our view of our situations may have had more to do with this anxiety than we think.

If the novel is instrument of insecurity and solitude, it is also an instrument of *regret*. How often in novels is the protagonist who has not won his or her narrative agon doomed to live out beyond the end of the novel an existence of trivial compensation and repression, severed from the thread of meaning the conflict of the plot offered? A character in what we might define as the novel of loss is deserted, abandoned, by the novel and by us, as the novel ends: there is no further interest in following the fate of someone who has failed to shape their destinies in a meaningful way. But even in a novel with a "happy ending" there is a similar feeling of abandonment. The hero or heroine wins what has been set out to be won, but what awaits now is a banality that by definition cannot match the intensity of the narrative triumph the character has gained. The novel ends, and the implication is that there is no need to pursue our interest in the protagonist any longer, because he or she has been entirely revealed by the narrative nodes the novel has enacted: the character of the hero holds for us no other engrossing mysteries.

Typically, the most successful metaphysical attitude the character of a novel can hope for is one variety or another of resignation. One is resigned to one's fate, to its bleakness, its future uneventfulness, but in truth this resignation is usually the resignation of defeat, of disappointed hopes, or, at best, the realization that one's previous hopes were unrealistic. The opposite of this practical stoicism is as sad; it is a kind of opulent, mindless cessation of striving. The character may have "succeeded," but what awaits now has something about it of the rich man's tedious retirement. The character will now presumably have the ease to reflect on the meaning of the narrative of his or her life, but we are aware that what really awaits is boredom and restlessness.

As heroes of our own existential novel, are we doomed ourselves to such inevitable disappointment, to a descent into non-meaning, or at best a self-forgetting? If the basic image of ourselves our culture offers us is so preponderantly this narrative, novelistic sense of ourselves, and if there seem to be so many limitations inherent in it, mightn't we be justified in asking ourselves whether there are alternative ways of conceiving the uses to which our lives are put?

Simone Weil has an essay in which she speculates on "the needs of the soul." She proposes such predictable matters as order, liberty, and security, and being Simone Weil, she also proposes such unexpected needs as obedience, and hierarchy. Strangely enough, perhaps because her concerns were so determined by the social crises of her moment, or perhaps because she thought it would be implicit in her ethical speculations, she never mentions beauty as one of the soul's needs. It's my feeling that the need for beauty, for the particular formal beauties of art, has to be included as one of our spiritual needs; it may even be, in our age, the most crucial.

I'm not sure how I would specify this need for formal beauty. Sometimes I think I intuit the *concept* of beauty—not beauty itself—most acutely when it isn't available to me, when I'm depressed, or more, precisely, when I'm going through what I would call an aesthetic depression, when for whatever reason the arts lose their power and effect for me, when I turn restlessly from one book to another, one piece of music to another, without ever connecting, without ever feeling the gratifying capture of my intellect, my senses, and the voice of my consciousness of a successful aesthetic occasion. Naturally these depressions will always be involved with other facts of my life. Its roots will have worldly reasons, love, grief, money, self-nonappreciation; in narrative terms, it will seem as though my self-making has faltered or gone awry. But at some point, all reasons, all conditions, fall away, and what I'm left with is the simple terrible fact that the beautiful has been forbidden to me.

When, for whatever reason, I come to the end of my depression, I occasionally realize that what happened to me wasn't entirely my fault. Because beauty in its relations with us is difficult, it is unreliable, ready to disappoint us. If we don't arrive at our aesthetic engagements in the proper state of mind, we will feel let down, jilted; we will seem to behold simulacra, shells of beauty that are like ghosts: cold, refusing to live and burn for us as we know they can.

A while ago I attended a colloquium on "Philosophy and Literature." Three philosophers and three literary critics, the "high" variety, respected, brilliant, and serious, participated in the discussion. The conversation was complex and witty; if it was inconclusive, we all assumed it would be because this kind of theme would by its nature generate no ultimate conclusion. I enjoyed the mental gymnastics, but I noticed several odd things: first, that all the speakers without exception spoke of literature as a moral implement, a somewhat less rigorous and trustworthy version of analytic philosophy, whose main contribution to human experience is its suppleness as an instrument of psychological investigation. Then, that what all the participants meant by "literature," was the novel, period; poetry was never mentioned. And last, that neither the word nor the phenomenon of beauty was ever brought up. The theme and the end of the conversation was rationality: by rationality was meant moral inquisitiveness, along with an implied commitment to some unspecified actions that would have as their ultimate consequences various genres of social betterment.

There is no question that we live in an age in which though there hasn't quite been a triumph of reason—there seems to be really no more reasonableness or sanity in the world than at any other moment—there does seem to have been a clear victory of, and an overwhelming faith in, rational technique, of all sorts, in every domain. This is nothing new: it is a development that, for good and ill, began with some of our beloved humanistic Greeks. But never before has this perspective been quite so pervasive, and quite so unquestioned. Even our most serious thinkers seem to have come to believe that all productive mental experience is fundamentally technical, "scientific" in one way or another. There is implicit in almost all of the serious mental activity of our age the belief that only intellection can approach the essence of anything, and that intellection itself is trustworthy only insofar as it entails a kind of analytic scrupulousness, which like a dentist's drill will decompose anything with which it is brought into contact.

The impetus behind this attitude isn't in itself ungenerous. On the contrary, as Dostoyevsky puts it (albeit sarcastically), "Our science seeks to explain what life is and strives to understand it in order to teach others to live." In the case of dedicated intellectuals this attitude has certainly been taken to heart. Whether the project is illusory, or even spiritually destructive, is another question, but what I want to point out here is that this arguably altruistic attitude seems to leave little time or space in the spirit for anything else, especially something so amorphous and undefinable as beauty. If you are involved in the salvation of the world—surely an engrossing, admirable project—any distraction that requires an intense involvement of the mind and will, such as the pursuit of formal art, becomes at best incidental, in some ways possibly even sinful. Reason, technical or not, has little to do with such an imprecise matter as beauty, and sometimes it seems with anything besides mind beholding with satisfaction its own workings as it probes and palpates and issues diagnoses and prescriptions.

If all this sounds rather joyless and grim, I believe it is. Were we to be considering an individual with a similarly undeviating self-focus and megalomaniacal self-estimation, we would feel we were speaking of a political fanatic, or of someone operating under the burden of clinical despair. It has occurred to me to imagine whether all of the critics and intellectuals around us who have given over all but the most cursory and reflexive commitment to formal beauty, might in truth be just that: victims of a cultural despair whose roots are so obscure and whose effects so general that they aren't even aware of the fact they are operating in an unimaginably desolate spiritual universe.

The result of this joylessness, this desolation, among literary critics and scholars is that a suspicion has arisen that literature is not a serious enough means to inquire into crucial issues of thought and life, and even into literature itself. So much of what is taught now in English departments isn't literature at all, but varieties of philosophy or sociology or outmoded political-economic theory, which attempt to bridge some undefinable ground between the literary object and critical speculation. It should hardly be surprising, though it can be terribly dismaying, that we end up with such dubious disciplines as "media studies," and classes that consist of teacher and students meditating upon such brilliant cultural personages as the Simpsons, or Beavis and Butthead, with the kind of attention they would have once given *Paradise Lost.*

But perhaps I'm not being entirely fair here. It wasn't, after all, professors of English who have brought about the general neglect of poetry over the last generations, or not intentionally. There is no question that poetry doesn't occupy the place it once did in the experience of even the relatively sophisticated general reader, and it's probably likely that even the specialists have turned away, perhaps unconsciously, from so marginalized an art form.

The reasons for the disregard of poetry are complicated. I've conducted an informal poll over the last years among people I know who are intellectuals but not in the field of literature, asking them whether they read poetry, and if not, why not.

Nearly all confessed to not ordinarily reading poetry, and the reason they inevitably gave was that poetry was too "hard": they all shared the belief that poetry required some special skill for its decipherment, not to speak of its appreciation, and this perception was almost always a response to how they had been taught poetry.

Over the last several generations, college English teachers have dutifully, often enthusiastically, taught the poetry of modernism to their students. At first, this seemed healthy. There had been for a long while a trend to teach literature almost entirely as literary history: certainly the study of poetry that was more contemporary, more germane to students' actual experience, was a beneficial antidote to this archaeological pedagogy. The problem was that the poets who became models for the study of modernist poetry were, indeed, its "difficult" poets, particularly Eliot, Pound, and Stevens. Often these poets' work was taught as a genre of arcane religious speculation or of philosophy. The poems of Eliot especially, with their apparently "irrational" organization, the dropping of transitional material between themes, the use of intense, "dreamlike" figuration, and the collagelike accumulation of apparently unorganized bits of language, were presented to the students as puzzles that had to be analyzed and explained. More crucially, and more disastrously, they were acclaimed as *the* poems of the current literary epoch. Students were thus taught to believe—I myself was, so I know it's true—that reading a poem was something that required training, and discipline, before it could be undertaken.

There's a terrific irony in this. The fact is that the majority of modernist poets were trying to accomplish precisely the opposite: they were trying to rejuvenate poetry, to take it back from the preceding generations, which had allowed a wistful nostalgia to become the propulsive emotion in their poetry. The poems the self-consciously modernist poets were writing asked for a different kind of response, but not a more laborious one. Rather they were seeking in the reader a release, a giving over of the poetic response to more immediately sensuous aspects of consciousness, those that react unself-consciously to metaphor, to the unpredictable movement of mind through language, and to the pure aural music of words.

In many countries, the poets of modernism had great popular

success, despite their apparent violation of old norms of literary decorum. Among many others, Prevert, Aragon, Apollinaire, and Desnos in France; Seferis and Ritsos in Greece; Neruda in Chile, and Lorca and Hernandez in Spain all had large audiences for their work, and some became popular cultural heroes.

What a pity that William Carlos Williams didn't become for the academy in America the prototype of the modern poet, rather than Eliot, with those disingenuous, deceptive, and finally destructive notes to *The Waste Land,* or Stevens, with, to young students at least, his difficult philosophical speculations. There is no question that Eliot and Stevens were major poets, great poets, their work is undeniably inspiring to readers who are experienced in poetry, but it can be terribly forbidding to even the best-intentioned but uninitiated student. Williams's poems are in their way as adventuresome as Eliot's, as sophisticated as Stevens, but they can be grasped with no recourse to explication and explanation. One of my favorite of Williams's poems begins as forthrightly as any short story:

> The pure products of America
> go crazy—
> mountain folk from Kentucky
>
> or the ribbed north end of
> Jersey
> with its isolate lakes and
>
> valleys, its deaf-mutes, thieves
> old names
> and promiscuity between
>
> devil-may-care men who have taken
> to railroading
> out of sheer lust of adventure—
>
> and young slatterns, bathed
> in filth
> from Monday to Saturday
>
> to be tricked out that night
> with gauds
> from imaginations which have no

peasant traditions to give them
character
but flutter and flaunt

sheer rags—succumbing without
emotion
save numbed terror

under some hedge of choke-cherry
or viburnum—
which they cannot express— . . .

A poem of enormous complexity, it deals with themes touch-
ing sociology, psychology, political-economic organization, in-
nocence, guilt, the recourse of human beings to nature; and yet
it needs no apparatus of explication, the voice captures us not by
its erudition, its hermeticism, but by its clarity, its self-conscious
musicalization of the colloquial. Though it uses some of the
devices of the Modern—particularly the dropping of some con-
nective tissue—its slight jumps in attention seem perfectly ordi-
nary: it moves as consciousness itself moves, without caring to
pay attention to its shifts of focus.

Williams and the many other more immediately accessible
American and English poets of the century remained neglected
in universities, at least until very recently, and the result was that
generations of students have come to mistrust poetry, to be
frightened of it, and to have no idea that the vast majority of
poems written in this century, and any century, require no erudi-
tion nor special knowledge.

There is one way, though, in which poetry can seem less
accessible than narrative prose: it is harder to find poems that
suit us, to which we can respond immediately and enthusiasti-
cally. Beginning a novel, one can be relatively certain, perhaps
because of our hunger for narrative, that unless there is some-
thing very off-putting about the style or the content of the book,
one will be caught by it. With poetry, in which the reading
experience is more focused, more intense, and more intimate,
this isn't always the case.

Not every poem fits every reader at every moment. You have
to be ready to encounter a poem: there's a *meeting* that has to be
induced between the text and the reader. The experience of the

beauty of poetry is relatively aggressive: it demands an engage-
ment, an exertion. This isn't to say, to repeat, that there's any
arcane initiation ritual to be undergone, it's just that we have to
expect that the mind will be more selective when it is asked to
respond in the more active way that poetry asks of us, and that is
one of its rewards. It is like music in this. Nearly any adolescent
will respond to nearly any popular music, but if you wish to
introduce a young person to classical music, which requires a
more complex attention, one must assume there is going to be
some groping through the tradition before the right music will
be encountered: some young people will be taken by the great
crashes of Romantic music, some by the intricate stitching of
Bach.

Poetry is usually taught as though every poem was accessible
to every student. And every poem is, if what we mean by acces-
sible is a diligent "understanding": every student is theoretically
capable of getting an 'A' in explicating a poem. If our wish,
though, is to have students respond deeply to poems, to make
them part of themselves, part of their cultural identity, we have
to be ready to allow them to pick and choose, to reject poems
that don't beckon to them. Which is what happens with every-
one, even experienced lovers of poetry, even poets. The most
avid reader of poems knows that all poems aren't always acces-
sible; it can depend on the day, or the decade. On a more
general level, the evolution of style, shifts in taste, the valuing of
one poet or one poetic epoch over another are all more exalted
instances of readers' need to find poems they love, and so to
make their own canons.

It would be disingenuous of me not to admit, though, that
beyond all of this, poetry is more difficult than the novel, maybe
even more than the other formal arts. A genuine experience of
any art, if it is authentic, is demanding: formal beauty demands
engagement, mental exertion, serious revision of habitual expec-
tation. Beauty isn't easy, otherwise it simply isn't beauty. And per-
haps it shouldn't be; perhaps if beauty were too accessible, too
constant, too faithful, we might come to disvalue it. The occa-
sional museum-goer's mild digestion of a blockbuster show's
taped art-appreciation lecture on a walkman is, we all suspect, to
be mistrusted. There are ways to consume paintings that have
nothing to do with the beauty of painting: we have a hunger for

image as well as for narrative, and a painting can be merely a picture, an illustration, and nothing more. Similarly music can serve as a pleasant distraction, white noise, more engrossing than the ordinary sounds of reality, but not in essence different from them.

Poetry is unique in that it can't be misused this way. Poetry demands an engagement that simply can't be simulated. If you are not in a state of awareness when you read a poem, if you are not at least minimally conscious of the poem's form, you are not really reading it. We can't fool ourselves with a poem, we can't let ourselves believe we're experiencing it when we're not. Our ease with any particular poem comes out of our familiarity with it or with others like it; it is an *earned* response, although both experienced readers of poetry and children before they learn to mistrust their responses don't have to be sensible of the concentration their minds have effected to arrive at that response.

Poetry can be difficult in other ways as well, especially in our age. The poetry of our time is still in some ways enacting the late-Romantic aesthetic project of incorporating and redeeming the apparently banal, the apparently ugly, even the apparently evil, into the realm of the beautiful. The content of poems over the last century has not always been attractive: on the contrary, from Baudelaire's rotting corpses, to Robert Lowell's obsessive recounting of his psychic infirmities, poetry has often taken on unlovely and morally arduous themes. This has been one of the merits of the poetry of our age, but it can also seem to deflect toward banality and chaos the very energy art presumably devotes to the sublime. This is a superficial perception, though: the basic business of poetry, the moving of content through form, the lifting of language and subject toward a condition of music, has not changed in the West since Homer and Archilochos. It is true, though, that what is demanded from poetry's complex beauty varies from age to age, and within an age. There are moments when the simplest, almost nearly wordless uttering of a line of a verse, recording nothing more than the flash of light on water, or expressing a seemingly self-evident metaphoric relation, can throb with meaning. It is as though all the world of spirit needs at moments such as this is a release; the soul can be renewed by the most primitive, nearly inarticulate song. At other times, poetry itself can seem to become tired: its music becomes slack, indolent, its vision amputated. It can give over too much of its responsibilities to other modes of expression. Then poetry has to be forced again to "raid the inarticulate," to make forays in active, aggressive ways into other vocabularies and other cultural nomenclatures. Poetry then can seem to be crude, overly aggressive, even, as in some modernist schools, violent. Sometimes, too, it can become more intellectual, recondite in its confrontations with meaning, with the content, the perceptions, the sentiments, it is trying to draw into its music. These are not necessarily changes that happen over long periods of literary time, or across significant cultural boundaries. They can, and do, occur in a much more rapid oscillation, within a single literary epoch, even within the work of a single poet. In Emily Dickinson's later poems, it seems to happen within the movements of the poems themselves: the most complicated analytical perceptions are driven toward resolution in the purest imagery, generating sometimes a mix of dazzling clarity with daunting density.

The potential reader, then, will often be off-balance in intuiting how to approach a poem. Disappointment lurks much more menacingly in the reading of poetry than in the other arts. For the experienced reader, though, this sense of disorientation, of surprise, is one of the primary expectations of reading poetry. To be confronted, shocked, to understand that a poem might demand a revision of the one's notion not only of the poem one is reading, but of poetry itself, becomes an elemental pleasure.

But to speak of the "pleasures" of poetry doesn't do justice to its seductive power. There is something almost immoderate in the way people become devoted to poetry: people *live* by poetry in a way they don't with the narrative arts. Poetry attaches itself to consciousness in a way no other language experience does. A poem can ferociously absorb the mind and the emotions: it resides in consciousness and becomes an entirely different resource than does narrative.

As we all know, a novelist's enactments of human conflicts can be probing and grandly comprehensive, the novel can educate the spirit wonderfully, but a novel is never as *conclusive* as a poem is, it cannot by its nature stay in memory the way a poem does, and consequently it cannot sustain the spirit in the same way.

I'll give an example. We have all read countless stories and novels about the breakdown of relationship between men and women, but I know none that has that sense of conclusiveness, of definitiveness, as does "The Hill Wife" by Robert Frost. The poem tells the story of a young wife who isn't able to bear the solitary rural existence to which she has been destined by her marriage. It is told in a series of short lyrics, some in the voice of the woman, some in a narrator's. In the last section of the poem, entitled "The Impulse," what the woman has been inarticulately trying to express to herself and to her husband becomes undeniably clear, with fateful results.

> It was too lonely for her there,
>   And too wild,
> And since there were but two of them,
>   And no child,
>
> And work was little in the house,
>   She was free,
> And followed where he furrowed field,
>   Or felled tree.
>
> She rested on a log and tossed
>   The fresh chips,
> With a song only to herself
>   On her lips.
>
> And once she went to break a bough
>   Of black alder.
> She strayed so far she scarcely heard
>   When he called her—
>
> And didn't answer—didn't speak—
>   Or return.
> She stood, and then she ran and hid
>   In the fern.
>
> He never found her, though he looked
>   Everywhere,
> And he asked at her mothers' house,
>   Was she there.
>
> Sudden and swift and light as that
>   The ties gave,
> And he learned of finalities
>   Beside the grave.

The woman's departure is as dramatic and poignant as anything in fiction. Besides the terrific compression of the poem, though, which so amplifies the effects of its symbolic markers, and beyond the awful rhythmic thuds with which those two-beat lines nail down the inevitability and irrevocability of what has happened, there's something that has made me feel every time I've read it a response much more complicated than the narrative itself would evoke. There's a feeling of duration, of lastingness, to the poem that goes beyond its plot, and the suffering of its characters. Despite that terrible "finalities" in the last stanza, the man and woman seem to continue to partake of an energy greater than the mere recounting of their agon. A novel, or a story in prose generally pretends to resolve the narrative of a character's trial; it rarely does, though, because the story of our real lives can't be completed until we are dead, until the last blink of consciousness leaves us. The characters in the Frost poem don't pretend to the same kind of resolution, or to any ultimate resolution. But still, the characters don't fade the way figures in novels do: somehow their presence resonates, echoes, goes on along with us in a special way.

When I used the expression a moment ago, "every time I've read . . ." the poem, I hardly remarked it myself, because that, after all, is what we know we do with poems. But it's in this, I think, where the closeness we feel to poems, to their content and their themes, resides. This repetition, this going over the poem again and again, makes the woman and the man in the Frost poem, as an instance, continue to exist with an unlikely vividness just because of their being repeated again and again, in exactly those words, with exactly those rhythms, those rhymes, those tiny efficient stanzas which so terribly and wonderfully contain them.

Perhaps it is this quality of repetition, of recurrence, of essences being relived, that is at the base of a formal nonnovelistic sense of life. Though the characters of novels become emblems for us, segments of the lenses of our moral reflection, our reading of poems is finally more mysterious, and more compelling. Poems are not written merely to be read, as novels are. A poem is meant to be read again and again, to be run through the mind until it is part of the mind, until the mind recites it as it recites itself. We tell poems to ourselves until both their rhythms, their forms, and their meanings find, or perhaps create, a place in our *voices,* rather than our minds. So we find sometimes we have memorized passages of poems without having tried to. Poetry shares with music this astonishing quality of moving through our perceptions and our mind to a place in us beyond either, a place which participates concretely in both consciousness and sense.

Mind becomes doubled in its dealings with the formal arts. We aren't satisfied to "know" a poem, a painting, or a piece of music by being able to describe it to ourselves, to paraphrase it. There has to be the incorporation of the actual object, of the precise notes in a piece of music, or the precise words in a poem, so that we hear the music or the poem when we think it, so that we hear our own actual voice, the voice we speak our own lives with, drawn into and fused with their melodies and rhythms.

Of course poems offer material for moral reflection just as novels do. They have to deal with the same themes, because there are not for human beings all that many themes. Poems seem to deal with these issues less comprehensively, less exhaustively than novels, but this is deceptive. Because what a poem might have to sacrifice in the accumulation of details, of surface subtlety, it more than makes up for in the intensification the form of the poem effects. It is one of the more profound mysteries of the mind that the struggle with form, which we have seen is defined by seemingly arbitrary necessities, actually enriches the expressiveness and effect of content. The double movement of willing consciousness toward form and expression enacts a struggle beyond anything that is happening in the matter of the poem, and the capacity of mind for self-distancing, for standing aside from itself and regarding itself, is obliterated by the force of this struggle.

It is also our sense of this struggle that attaches us to the poet, as much as to what a poem is saying. When we read a novel, our sense of its author manipulating from behind the scenes drifts in out of our awareness; we can be curious about why the author's character may have generated such and such manifestations of itself, but, unless we know the novelist, this is quite incidental. This is not the case with a poet. In the struggle toward form, what happened to the poet in the creation of the poem happens again in the here and now of our reading of the poem; the impulse toward form, our feeling of its successful attainment, is absolutely critical to experience of reading poetry. What the poet has undergone in contending with form is not something that happens to the poem's content; rather it is the poet's actual self, his or her ultimate reality, that is the material of the poem's artifice. There is a self-making involved in this struggle, but it is of a radically different sort from that which afflicts the characters, and, as we have seen, possibly the readers of novels.

Poetry induces mind into involving itself entirely into an awareness of its formal striving, and in doing so it demands that mind realize as much as it can its entire nature, not only its intellectual or moral capacity. The poem offers the mind—the soul, we could probably say now—a way to experience itself objectively, by participating in something that both draws it beyond its own spiritual capabilities and still refers in the most concrete way to these capabilities.

These involvements, these intensities, these movements of the poem into the voice of consciousness help explain why to those who are attached to it poetry is an implement of the moral imagination every bit as efficient as the novel, and whose potential effects are even more profound. Just as the form of poetry reinforces expression, it also focuses and fortifies the impulse toward resolution, toward definitiveness, in our spiritual reflections. The *beauty* the poem devises, enacts, elicits in us is essential to our moral nature just because it cannot be contained in any ethical system or moral code: it certifies to us that there is something within our potential that goes beyond our ability simply to think about things, to reason our way through our experience; beauty proves to us that there are ways out of the circularities through which we reasonably examine our narratives, and narratively try to comprehend our self-reasoning.

I think of Simone Weil again in this. Weil was one of the most rational products of our very rational culture. Her erudition was unquestionable; her technical philosophical equipment so acute, so integrated into her character and thought, that we hardly notice it. And yet, her most profound and most enduring spiritual experience occurred as she stood in a chapel in southern France, and recited to herself a poem by George Herbert.

To her astonishment and gratitude she suddenly arrived at a palpable realization of a religious conviction that had long eluded her, and she became convinced as she never had been of the accessibility of the realm of the spirit. The poem is "Love," one of Herbert's painfully poignant, sometimes shocking poems of the exigencies of faith.

> Love bade me welcome: yet my soul drew back,
>   Guilty of dust and sin.
> But quick-eyed Love, observing me grow slack
>   From my first entrance in,
> Drew near to me, sweetly questioning,
>   If I lacked anything.
>
> A guest, I answered, worthy to be here:
>   Love said, You shall be he.
> I the unkind, ungrateful? Ah my dear,
>   I cannot look on thee.
> Love took my hand, and smiling did reply,
>   Who made the eyes but I?
>
> Truth Lord, but I have marred them: let my shame
>   Go where it doth deserve.
> And know you not, says Love, who bore the blame?
>   My dear, then I will serve.
> You must sit down, says Love, and taste my meat:
>   So I did sit and eat.

But perhaps it's not proper to emphasize too much the moral function of poetry, as though the last word on poetry had to have to do with its usefulness, its ethical rather than its aesthetic potential. The closest relative of poetry isn't philosophy or religion, but music; its grandeur is artistic, the way it touches us, the pure stirrings it evokes in us, have primarily to do with beauty, with the radiance beauty brings us in itself, beyond whatever sentiments it uses for its embodiment. The content of *The Marriage of Figaro* clearly is not essential to the joy we feel when we listen to it; the religious doctrines Bach incarnated in his masses and cantatas is interesting to us, but they are not at the center of our pleasure; they have nothing to do with the rapture his music brings us, nor with the sense of relief we even feel when we listen that we are somehow now as we should be, that this, this rapt attentiveness, this feeling of something within us flooding through us, is what our human nature really is.

From Chaucer to Shakespeare, from Keats to Hopkins to Yeats to our contemporaries, poetry is there for us in the same way, bringing us, if we give ourselves to it, the same realization and exaltation. And the cadences and metaphoric ingenuities of contemporary poetry can offer us as much radiant pleasure, as much the sense that we are experiencing ourselves in a way that opens us out beyond ourselves, rather than merely condemning us to reexperiencing the strictures of our amputated narratives, the inescapable defining of our lives by the stories of our history.

Here is recent a poem by Robert Pinsky, "Shirt." Listen as Pinsky moves his sinuous cadences and rollicking feeling for the musical palpability of words from the most banal consideration of one of the most banal objects in life, an ordinary shirt, to a touching scene of death by fire through economic rapacity, to the poetry of Hart Crane, to a consideration of historical social illusions and workers' struggles in Scotland, then, in the un-likeliest leap, to George Herbert and his namesake in a textile factory, and back again to the shirt.

The back, the yoke, the yardage. Lapped seams,
The nearly invisible stitches along the collar
Turned in a sweatshop by Koreans or Malaysians

Gossiping over tea and noodles on their break
Or talking money or politics while one fitted
This armpiece with its overseam to the band

Of cuff I button at my wrist. The presser, the cutter,
The wringer, the mangle. The needle, the union,
The treadle, the bobbin. The code. The infamous blaze

At the Triangle Factory in nineteen-eleven.
One hundred and forty-six died in the flames
On the ninth floor, no hydrants, no fire escapes—

The witness in a building across the street
Who watched how a young man helped a girl to step
Up to the windowsill, then held her out

Away from the masonry wall and let her drop.
And then another. As if he were helping them up
To enter a streetcar, and not eternity.

A third before he dropped her put her arms
Around his neck and kissed him. Then he held
Her into space, and dropped her. Almost at once

He stepped to the sill himself, his jacket flared
And fluttered up from his shirt as he came down,
Air filling up the legs of his gray trousers—

Like Hart Crane's Bedlamite, "shrill shirt ballooning."
Wonderful how the pattern matches perfectly
Across the placket and over the twin bar-tacked

Corners of both pockets, like a strict rhyme
Or a major chord. Prints, plaids, checks,
Houndstooth, Tattersall, Madras. The clan tartans

Invented by mill-owners inspired by the hoax of Ossian,
To control their savage Scottish workers, tamed
By a fabricated heraldry: Mac Gregor,

Bailey, Mac Martin. The kilt, devised for workers
To wear among the dusty clattering looms.
Weavers, carders, spinners. The loader,

The docker, the navvy. The planter, the picker, the sorter
Sweating at her machine in a litter of cotton
As slaves in calico headrags sweated in fields:

George Herbert, your descendant is a Black
Lady in South Carolina, her name is Irma
And she inspected my shirt. Its color and fit

And feel and its clean smell have satisfied
Both her and me. We have culled its cost and quality
Down to the buttons of simulated bone,

The buttonholes, the sizing, the facing, the characters
Printed in black on neckband and tail. The shape,
The label, the labor, the color, the shade. The shirt.

The shirt, indeed, transfigured now with all this history and
all this unforgettable formal dexterity, grace, and efficiency into
pure inspiration: matter, form, beauty—the poem.

UNDER DISCUSSION
David Lehman, General Editor
Donald Hall, Founding Editor

Volumes in the Under Discussion series collect reviews and essays about individual poets. The series is concerned with contemporary American and English poets about whom the consensus has not yet been formed and the final vote has not been taken. Titles in the series include: